Books by T. Berry Brazelton, M.D.

INFANTS AND MOTHERS
TODDLERS AND PARENTS
ON BECOMING A FAMILY
DOCTOR AND CHILD
TO LISTEN TO A CHILD
WORKING AND CARING

WORKING
&
CARING

A Merloyd Lawrence Book

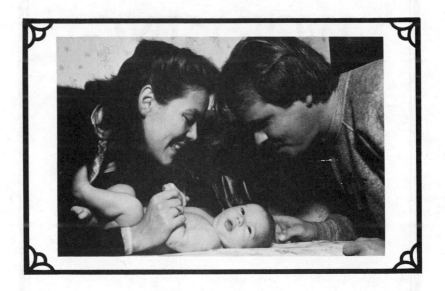

ADDISON-WESLEY PUBLISHING COMPANY, INC.
Reading, Massachusetts · Menlo Park, California
Don Mills, Ontario · Wokingham, England · Amsterdam
Sydney · Singapore · Tokyo · Mexico City · Bogota
Santiago · San Juan

WORKING
&
CARING

T. Berry Brazelton, M.D.

All photographs in this book were taken by Alexandra Dor-Ner.

Excerpt from *Changing* by Liv Ullman, copyright © 1983 by Alfred Knopf, Inc., is reprinted with the kind permission of the publisher.

Library of Congress Cataloging-in-Publication Data

Brazelton, T. Berry, 1918–
　Working and caring.

　"A Merloyd Lawrence book."
　Bibliography: p.
　Includes index.
　1. Parenting—United States—Case studies.　2. Children of working parents—United States—Case studies.　3. Mothers—Employment—United States—Case studies.　4. Married people—Employment—United States—Case studies.　5. Parent and child—United States—Case studies.　I. Title.
HQ755.8.B73　1985　　649'.1　　85-11189
ISBN 0–201–10623–X

Cover design by Janis Capone
Jacket photo by Hornick/Rivlin Studio
Text design by Diana Eames Esterly

Set in 10 point Barcelona Book by DEKR Corporation, Woburn, Massachusetts

ABCDEFGHIJ-DO-898765
First printing September 1985

To Merloyd, my editor,
supporter and dear friend

ACKNOWLEDGMENTS

I would like to thank all the working parents in my practice who have participated in this book—gathering material, criticizing and enriching my ideas. They have made me realize that working in the marketplace is no harder than being a parent at home, but that doing both doubles the hours, the roles, the worries and the joys. These families have enhanced my life in every way.

Dear Linn,

There were so many demands from the outside, people who wanted part of that time we should have had together. You have been alone with what we had looked forward to sharing between us.

You have had a hectic and stressed mamma who gives you quick hugs. Listens to you, while she drums her fingers impatiently on the table.

I have been tired and asked you not to be persistent with me, because my nerves were on edge.

And I have seen you at times withdraw from me.

Been afraid to call you back. Afraid because my bad conscience has weighed upon me.

Afraid because the exterior success I have had was achieved at the cost of something the two of us might have had together.

Most afraid I am that it will be too late to reach you on the day I can give you all my time.

You shall know that I love you all the time.

Through the years I have struggled with my profession. Tried to find out who I am and why I am.

Your thin little body is as close to life as I have come.

You who are life itself when I touch you and you become heavy and warm and lean against me. When you pat my cheek and say: "Little Mamma," and understand more than I realize.

When you say that I must not be sad, because you are there.

When you make my life richer, just by being.

Dear Linn . . .

From Changing
by Liv Ullman

Contents

xiii

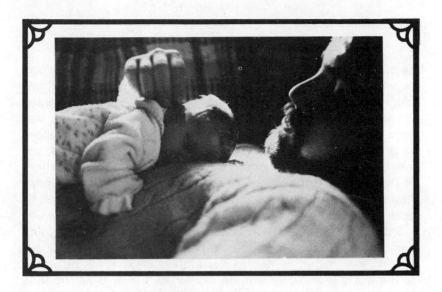

INTRODUCTION

Families Without a Culture

Not long ago, a mother I'd never seen before entered my office with her five-month-old son. As she came in, she said, "Doctor, should I wean my baby?"

I thought to myself, What an odd way to greet a new doctor. "Why do you ask?" "I have to go back to work," she said, as if it were a threat. When I asked her when, she said, "In the next few months." Relieved, I said brightly, "Certainly not, then! Just get him used to a bottle in the middle of the day. Plan to breast-feed him before and after work. You'll find it's so great to come home at the end of the day and be able to put him right to breast. You feel cemented to each other all over again."

At this, she sat down in my easy chair, clutching her baby closer, and began to cry. I was horrified. I thought I must have said the wrong thing to this woman I hardly knew. Brushing the tears away, she explained her feelings. "I hoped you'd say that. I haven't been able to hear it from anyone else. I'm a lawyer in town. Suddenly, I don't want to go back to work at all. I was counsel for a women's rights organization and had bought completely into their beliefs. I waited as long as I dared to have this baby, though we both wanted him. I love my work and resented the idea of having to leave it for even a month. After he was born, I suddenly fell completely in love. I couldn't eat or sleep or think of anything but my baby. I don't care about work any longer. I realize I'm a woman without a culture. I can't believe in the women's movement in the same way I did in the past. And I have no good models to follow as a mother who must go back to work."

This woman's plea for help, her need for understanding, and her need to understand her own passionate feelings about becoming a nurturer, as well as her ambivalence about returning to the workplace, is a common cry today. I hear it all the time in my practice. Women feel that they must do one or the other, that they can't do both well. They can't be good mothers and successful working women at the same time. A common myth now is that one must be a superwoman to accomplish both tasks—a "supermom" at home and a "super success" at work. This "splitting apart" is very painful for most women, and they are setting impossible goals in each area, as if to make up for the conflict they feel. This mother's cry for a "new culture" led me to write this book. For here was a woman who was indeed a success both at mothering and at her job. Yet she felt as if she were a failure in both. I felt I must address her questions.

Most new fathers have not faced this kind of splitting apart. Many, however, will—as they begin to play a more nurturing role. My role is that of advocate for children, and, since I know children flourish best in nurturing families, I want to explore the feelings of both men and women as they attempt to divide themselves between two roles each.

Today, working couples with small children have five careers between them: two nurturing jobs, two in the workplace, and their relationship with one another. How, then, can they keep alive both their sense of pleasure and their sense of sharing? This is what this book is about. It is also about maintaining, in the middle of the tumult, a balance between the all-important needs of children and the ever-pressing demands of most jobs.

Each of the three families whose lives are woven throughout this book dramatizes this inevitable struggle. I have chosen a professional husband and wife, a single mother, and a blue-collar couple to show that the big questions—when to return to work, how to share the care, and how to handle the developmental hurdles of normal childhood when childbearing is not your only job—confront all working parents, whatever their circumstances.

There is passion in the struggle. This is fortunate, because it is our passion that provides us with the fuel to carry on. We know that working families are under pressure and that both parents have to learn to share the day-to-day household responsibilities and child care. What is more of a surprise to new parents is that this very sharing creates territorial and competitive issues. Anyone who cares about a small baby will compete with everyone else for that baby. Two involved, caring parents will inevitably become jealous of each other's ways of loving and raising that child. If this competition becomes energy for caretaking, if it spurs learning from the trial and error of two different approaches, it will provide a positive environment for the children in the family.

As I have said, trying to fill two roles adequately feels like being split in two. Erik Erikson once reminded me that, for any mother, the most difficult thing about having a *second* baby is her feeling that she can't split herself in two, that she doesn't have enough to give to both babies. Mothers who try to work and mother at the same time feel that way, too. They ask, Have I enough to go around? However, just as mothers learn they can love two children, so too does a genuine concern for both baby and job bring out in them new energy and abilities. This very upheaval, present in parents who try to split themselves in two, is a striking reminder of how much motivation and drive is really available for these two tasks.

A friend of mine is very successful at mothering her seven-month-old baby and at the same time running an exciting child welfare program. She told me she constantly shifts gears. When she's in one place, her mind wanders to the other, and vice versa. The more parents value each role, the more demanding is the split. And on top of this, social pressure to be a child development expert as well as a loving parent requires a kind of "supermom" or "superdad." Parents who ask this of themselves are not likely ever to have any fun. Since I know that a child needs a flexible, humorous parent more than a professional, I encourage parents throughout this book to let themselves enjoy the role of parenting.

Balancing work and child care is an issue for most parents today. By 1990, it is predicted that 75 percent of children will have both parents working outside the home. The pendulum has swung so far in the past forty years that now most mothers at home wonder if perhaps they should be working. There is the feeling that (1) unless she works, a woman is missing out on an important part of life and (2) taking care of children is not rewarding work. This creates unspoken pressures on women and makes every new mother who works wonder when she should return to her job. If she stays home, she feels that perhaps she should be doing something "more rewarding than caring for a baby." At each frustration, at each spurt in her baby's growing independence, she is likely to question whether the baby still needs her enough to balance her own need to return to work.

At the same time, there is a lingering, unspoken social bias against mothers who leave their babies, unless it is absolutely necessary. Every woman who leaves her child in another's care constantly wonders whether she is doing the right thing. In her mind, there is still the image of the "perfect mother" she ought to be—one who is at home taking care of her children. Hovering within is the nagging question, Is it really all right for me to work and mother at the same time? We need to tell these mothers that, at a certain age, babies get what they need from other caregivers and that they, the mothers, will be able to stand the separation without feeling too grieved at the loss.

Without such reassurance, mothers are at the mercy of a society that does not take into account the importance of either individual needs or those of the family. In Chapter 4, I outline what we now know about separation and timing one's return to work.

In the forties and fifties, the talents and personal aspirations of able women were ignored. Today we may be ignoring another deep-seated drive in women—a strong feeling that their primary responsibility is to nurture their children and their spouse. It may be unfair to expect a woman to be the fulcrum of her family; but it has always been so, and women feel it instinctively. To expect a woman to be successful both at home and in the work-place adds responsibility onto responsibility. Women are under fire these days. Conflicting pressures leave them in a painful bind—damned if they do and damned if they don't.

Can a woman decide to take on and competently carry out two roles at once? I certainly think so, and it seems time for us to face this fact as a national trend. It is important to figure out how it can be done so that our next generation of babies and their parents do not suffer.

We learn about ourselves as mature people in the process of being responsible for and nurturing a baby. Mothers who work must learn two very different approaches to life. Abraham Zaleznik in a speech given at the Harvard Business School said that these two approaches, which can never really be reconciled, will be different for each woman. In the workplace, a woman needs to be pragmatic, somewhat isolated emotionally, and forceful and direct in managing her job and those around her. She must be efficient. But an efficient woman could be the worst kind of mother for her children. For at home, a woman must be flexible, warm, and concerned; willing to experience and to learn from her failures, and open to change. She must always be ready for things to go wrong and be able to compensate. To be able to shift gears quickly and without too much anguish, from one approach to the other, may be the key to success in these two, very different roles.

In planning this book, I first saw the problem as one of "mothers who work." The working mothers of my small patients disabused me of that quickly. They said, "If you blame women for the problems that arise, you are ignoring a large part of the issue. It is not just a problem for women but for men, too. Men expect to work but most don't expect to help at home. And yet they must. The problem in a working family is that no one is there all the time to care for the children. Why not see it as a problem for 'working parents,' so that fathers too can see their roles as changing? Men must be more active in nurturing as well as at breadwinning. At least half the problem today is that men haven't been prepared well for their new roles. Women need to learn to do two jobs well, but so do men."

There is an increasing number of studies about the effect of father involvement on children's development in early infancy. Some of the most provocative ones demonstrate that children whose fathers were actively involved with them in their infancy enter school with higher IQs and a better chance for success in the future. But what is even more exciting, these children have better relationships with their peers, a better sense of humor, and appear to have a stronger self-image. In a father's involvement there are many opportunities to strengthen the child as well as the whole family. That shouldn't surprise any of us.

Research in our laboratory at Children's Hospital in Boston (with co-workers Suzanne Dixon, Michael Yogman, Edward Tronick, and Heidi Als) has demonstrated that the father of a small baby shows a very different yet predictable kind of behavior while playing with his infant. A father touches and pokes more. He is likely to speak and react in playful, stimulating ways that produce a heightened reaction in his baby. Whereas a mother will hold, soothe, and play gently with her baby, a father seems to respond differently. Very quickly (as early as the first month) babies demonstrate an expectancy for these playful responses. At one month, an infant's shoulders and eyebrows rise in an expression of expectant joy when father's voice is heard in the distance. The importance to the baby of this different, more playful response is already reflected in this behavior of joyful expectancy, which contrasts clearly with the more urgent and "hungry" expectancy for the mother. At one month, a baby with an actively involved father is already learning about two different kinds of people in the world.

Father involvement has indirect as well as direct effects on a new developing family. Working with the Brazelton Neonatal Behavioral Assessment Test, Judy Beal, R.N. showed that fathers become significantly more sensitive to their babies' cues if a professional points out a new baby's behavior to them on the second or third day of life. Dr. Ross Parke has also demonstrated the infant's amazing ability to respond, which allows the father to feel more confident of his own ability to nurture. Not only does a father's discovery of the rich behavioral repertoire of his newborn directly influence his own behavior, but also his increased participation indirectly affects the mother, who senses that he is more involved with her as well. She feels less depressed, less isolated, and more confident of her own sensitivity to her baby's behavior. By interacting with and learning more about their new baby, each parent reinforces the other.

Why has it taken so long as a society to begin actively to include fathers in the family's adjustment to a new baby? The new emphasis on father participation at delivery and in child-birth classes helps recruit fathers for a more involved role with their babies and wives at home. My hope is that these more involved and more motivated fathers will feel a kind of responsibility for baby and spouse that will serve to cement the endangered family structure in our society today.

This generation is a time of transition for men as well as women. The traditional breadwinning roles for men are being threatened as women prove themselves to be competent in the workplace. They manage, make decisions, and perform as well as men. When men see that women are capable of managing two roles successfully it uncovers an unconscious fear—that women really are the dominant sex. Freud's theory of penis envy has always seemed to me a reversal of a more obvious male emotion—the envy of a woman's capacity to conceive and produce another living being. Men are bound to be in awe of this and to be competitive at an unconscious level. As women prove their competence in the workplace as well, men are likely to be doubly threatened.

Freud also pointed out that, for all human beings, the basic requirements of human existence are love and work. If, as I try to suggest in this book, women can both work and nurture their families successfully, we men will have two options: either we identify with their efforts or we subside into ineffective territoriality and jealousy. Of course, my bias is clear. The opportunity for men to learn more about themselves and to grow, by fostering their nurturant sides, is obvious. But it isn't necessarily an easy task; nor do men receive much support for it before they become fathers. There is still a very strong cultural bias against a man actively tending to his family or making it his top priority. One father, who asked for and was granted leave to take care of his six-month-old baby when his wife returned to work, assured me that the other partners in his firm approved—at the time. Several of them congratulated him and stated that they wished they'd had the courage to take leave when their babies were small. But these same colleagues took over all his accounts, left him out of all discussions, and, when he returned, treated him like a novice. So unconscious was their put-down that they were extremely offended when he tried to point it out to them. He was not able to discuss it with them, and he felt subtly but firmly shut out of the club by the atmosphere in the office thereafter. He told me that he knew what women went through when they had to fight for time off from work to look after their families.

The learning process, which all new parents must go through, is particularly uncomfortable for men. The myth that women tend to know instinctively what to do in a child's crisis is deep-seated. Books on child care press a parent to react "naturally." Very few new parents, who have never been with small babies nor observed other parents with their infants, have any sense of what a "natural" reaction is. Men feel inadequate in the face of such advice, because they feel that it is women who really know what to do. Hence, the kind of learning and experimentation necessary to react "instinctively" is too often avoided by fathers. To abdicate to the mother seems an easy solution. Sometimes, though, there is no mother available. In that case, the experience of a father alone and responsible for his small baby, though alarming, is a priceless step toward confident parenting.

A father who allows himself to be excluded with no chance to feel competent and important to his baby will be angry and will often undermine his wife's role. On the other hand, a father who participates actively as a caregiver, learning from his mistakes and successes, will grow with his baby. There are few experiences in adult life more sobering and maturing than the trial-and-error rearing of a developing child.

On a national level, we need to back up symbolically the importance of father participation. I would like to see legislated a paid period of leave for fathers around the time of the birth of their baby. I would like to see industry respect the father's role in coping with a child's illness at home by granting him time off to spell his wife. In Chapter 4, I suggest some national priorities that could encourage father participation.

Men need more and more support and preparation to become successful nurturers. Boys need to be around babies and to be made to feel responsible for them. Adolescent males need to be incorporated into child-care settings and to be educated on early child development. We all need to see, as a cultural goal, the successful accomplishment of the two roles by all mature adults—men and women alike—both in the marketplace and, more important, at home, as nurturers for spouses and children. I hope fathers will feel supported by this book as they take on their new role in working families.

Role strain, especially around emergencies such as a new baby or an illness in the family, can be a sign that it's time to reevaluate the balances within the family. Job dissatisfaction can be compounded by crises at home. Family stress can in turn create job stress. Studies of working mothers show that women who are happy in their work are more likely to perceive the need for and to create higher values at home, and their children profit by it. In Part III I try to offer working parents some insights into the normal developmental periods in a child's life that inevitably place extra stress on parents. This stress can be more intense when both parents work. I hope that, by knowing ahead when these periods occur, working families can turn a normal stress into a learning experience.

What about the single parent? Fifty-eight percent of children in the United States will spend part of their childhood in a one-parent family. How can working single parents make it up to a baby? As I try to demonstrate in the story of Tina and her single mother, Alice, raising children alone is not an easy task. Both parent and child often feel the need for the alternative outlets that are naturally provided by the presence of a second parent. I hope that their story will help shore up working single parents along their lonely path. I admire those who face it bravely and successfully.

In this book I address another vital issue: the choice of a day-care center or other kind of child care while parents work. Each family I portray makes a different choice, and in Chapter 8, I lay out some guidelines for finding and evaluating day-care centers and caretakers in the home.

Finally, my intention is that this book demonstrate, with all the passion and caring that is involved, the conflict two working parents face as they carry out their five careers, and which single parents must face alone. I hope that, in these examples of day-to-day life in working families, the normal crises of childhood can be seen for what they are: opportunities for a parent's deeper understanding and reorganization of family life and personal goals. Thoughtful childrearing is critical not only for the future of our children but also for the happiness of their parents.

PART I

Paradise Lost

1

The Snows

Carla Snow is a successful lawyer in her mid-thirties. She had spent ten years in legal training and, during the last three years, has risen precipitously in the firm. The older partners of the firm, all men, had at first treated her like a "pretty child." But they soon came to respect her clear, incisive mind. The younger male members, who had flirted with her and in other ways had put her down, were surprised that "a good-looking woman could be successful in a man's game." They began to treat her like another man. This "compliment" took the place of earlier hostile reminders that she had only been hired to fill the firm's requirement to provide equal opportunity. She loved her work. Recently she was beginning to feel confident enough to dare to ask for maternity leave. She recognized the dangers in leaving her job, but she had to balance this fear against her growing desire to have a baby.

She and Jim have been married for five years and always planned to have a family. As her career blossomed she had found ways to rationalize one postponement after another. Jim is an accountant, moderately successful, and, proud of her success, had been entirely sympathetic to her decision to postpone pregnancy. Their life-style has rapidly escalated and they depend on both their salaries. Each year, having a baby had seemed like a bigger and bigger hurdle.

Carla was haunted by her age. She was getting older. Was she too old to be a mother? Could she be a *good* mother? As thirty-five loomed closer, she had felt the possibility of childbearing slip away from her. Had she been selfish to take this time "for herself," to solidify her career? On the other hand, she knows she has become a more secure person and she hopes it will make her a better mother.

    🔊 *Working women are in a bind these days. As they invest themselves in their jobs, their satisfaction in their work increases. As they begin to be accepted in the job market "not as a woman but as an equal," their sense of achievement is reinforced. But they still feel it is a precarious, ephemeral kind of adjustment. Carol Gilligan points out in* In Another Voice *that women still feel, at a very deep level, uncomfortable in competitive roles. The women's movement has not dispelled this feeling. There is, too, the sense that, if one should disappear from the job for a while, the toehold on the ladder of success will be lost forever. If one has achieved any success, the competitive feelings of the men and the other women will likely make reentry more difficult. Peers are often jealous of a woman's success both at home and in the workplace.*

    Many of these anxieties are real, but they also stem from the kind of self-questioning that women are doing now—if they have a choice between working and not working. Having that choice often makes it more difficult to justify working. Either way, whatever goes wrong seems to many women to be their own fault. Yet there are benefits for every member of the family when a woman feels fulfilled. Research clearly demonstrates that, if a woman is successful and happy at work, she is more likely to be successful at home, and as a mother. This fact can seem like a threat to men who may still feel that they cannot nurture and at the same time be successful at their jobs.

    Leaving a job in which one has proven oneself, in exchange for an unknown new role, can be frightening. The present trend is toward postponing parenthood until the thirties, which gives the decision a lot more weight. On the positive side, earlier role conflicts are likely to have been sorted out—for better or for worse. Decisions are clearer, less fraught with unresolved personal issues. By then, one is more mature, more aware of the responsibilities involved, and cares a lot more. On the other hand, the desire to do the "perfect" job makes the trial and error nature of childrearing more difficult for older parents. They see themselves as "giving up" a lot to become parents, and so they expect it to be more rewarding as well, which can put a burden on the children.

The age of thirty-five has become a turning point, fixed in people's minds because of a statistic. Women over thirty-five are statistically more likely to produce infants with certain congenital defects—Down syndrome, spinal defects, and other serious chromosomal disorders. However, these disorders can be diagnosed early in pregnancy by amniocentesis and other tests, and an impaired fetus can be aborted. Both older and younger women can be protected from delivering a severely handicapped baby. Women over thirty-five in good health can now consider themselves an excellent risk for a normal pregnancy.

Early Doubts

As soon as Carla and Jim decided to take the plunge into parenthood, doubts began to loom. Were they right to dare? Would they have a normal baby after all this time? It took several months for Carla to conceive. This surprised them. They had been so sure that, as soon as they wanted a baby, Carla would become pregnant. When several months had passed and no pregnancy had occurred, they thought one of them must be infertile. Then all their anxieties flooded over them at once. They had waited too long. They had been too selfish in wanting to get their careers started first. They were no longer fit to be parents. The urgency to have the baby became an obsession. They had to prove that none of this was true.

Finally, Carla had become pregnant—or at least she had missed a period and was beginning to feel queasy in the mornings. When tests verified Carla's pregnancy, she and Jim were both relieved and elated. They felt like new people—intact, family people! The cocktail circuit lost its sparkle. They only wanted to talk about themselves and the new adjustment they would have to make. Work seemed very secondary, all of a sudden.

Carla felt a glow every time she thought about it. When she felt nauseated, she exulted to think that it was because of her new baby growing inside of her. Jim began to treat her with awe. He helped her into her chair, opened doors for her, and watched her every move. If she wanted to eat something special, he had to decide whether it was "all right for the baby." She developed a craving for salty foods. He asked their friends whether salt was "okay for the baby." At first his concern and attention was fun, but it became an obsession. Carla found herself getting irritated at his primary concern for the baby. Her needs were secondary. Was this a sign of what was to come? She felt abandoned, the way she used to feel in the middle of the night when her father went off on a long business trip. As a child, she had made up an imaginary friend to replace him. She had long ago realized that Jim had taken this imaginary friend's place. And now she didn't want to give Jim up to anyone—not even to their baby.

As her initial euphoria wore off, Carla began to face—just a little—the reality of her new role. She looked at babies in carriages, imagining how it would be to care for them. She watched her friends who were mothers more closely—to see what they did with their babies, what it meant to them to be maternal and unselfish. Fears returned at night as she lay in bed. Could she ever be a real mother? Would she become sour, angry, and depressed like her own mother? Would Jim desert her as he turned to the baby? She had barely adjusted to being Jim's wife and had only begun to dare to trust him. Now she was endangering their relationship by getting pregnant.

During the day, Carla seemed just as cheerful as ever. It was exciting to be pregnant, and, for the most part, she felt great. But her work was beginning to suffer. How would it be when she had the baby? She dreamt of it at work. It took her twice as long to draft a letter. Her colleagues wondered until she finally told them she was pregnant. No one seemed surprised. In fact, everyone was delighted! Didn't they feel, as she felt, that she was deserting them? Didn't they notice that she was only half there, and would soon be useless to them?

Her mother expressed openly what others may have felt: "Well, dear, now you can stop proving yourself in the business world and begin to be a real woman. You can stop working and be a regular housewife, like the rest of us." This statement irritated Carla so much that she knew it had hit the mark. Was she afraid of this possibility, or did she long for it—or both? Should she decide right now whether to work or to mother? If she wanted to do both, was she being too ambitious and self-centered? All along she had sensed her mother's ambivalence about her work, especially her success at it.

≥ Younger women—and some older women—now have many opportunities for self-fulfillment in exciting new careers. This is bound to create ambivalence in those older women who had to deny any similar hopes in their lives. Carla may have to learn to be a working mother alone. She may not be able to share any guilty or angry feelings she may have with her mother. It may be difficult for her to do the work of pregnancy—to fantasize, to imagine herself as a mother.

In my book On Becoming a Family, *I describe some of the dreams and fantasies that are universal to the "work of pregnancy." Women who want to do a good job of mothering their new baby must go through this period of self-questioning. It is a period of turmoil, but a healthy one, which stirs up the energy a woman needs to meet the natural "crisis" of having a baby. This is when women wonder whether they can ever become a good enough parent, whether they can give up their present adjustment—often newly made—to take on such a responsibility. Often they revert back to their own experience in being mothered. Although many want to reject that experience as a model, it is important in preparing for their own role as a mother. If a working mother-to-be had a mother who was "at home," she must compare herself with that "womanly" person she remembers.*

A working mother-to-be spends a lot of time justifying to herself her need to work. She wonders whether she really wants to be pregnant at all and dreams about rejecting the fetus. If she weren't pregnant, life could be so simple again. Because these fantasies of rejection are intolerable to her, they may take the form of fears about having damaged her baby. She might dream of an impaired infant and how she would ever handle such a stress, or reconcile it with her working life.

I find in my own practice that pregnant women who know they will have to return to work early after a new baby do not dare to dream too passionately about their new role or think too much about the possibility of having a less-than-perfect baby. It is as if they are already guarding themselves against too much attachment, against the emotional work which prepares a women for both the utter joy and the devastating disappointment that might come with the new baby. This takes energy away from the work of attachment in pregnancy. A woman needs to dream about both roles and how they can be handled together. All eventualities need to be confronted in dreams and fantasies. This is a critical part of the work of pregnancy, of "getting ready."

Jim seemed elated. He spoke of nothing else when they were alone. They talked incessantly of "how it will be." She found herself getting jealous of him already. He seemed so sure of his role; she so unsure of hers. He had been on the phone to his parents and brothers boasting about "his baby." When they talked about work, she spoke of hers in the past tense. His future seemed clear; hers too cloudy to trust. She didn't dare to admit to these feelings of inadequacy, even to herself. Admission would be a surrender of some sort. She felt inadequate to handle both roles, and worried silently about which role she must give up.

Father-to-be

Jim was more successful at hiding his deeper concerns. He had always been an optimistic person, able to hide anxieties and conflicts behind a facade of self-assurance. He sensed Carla's brooding and realized that she was taking this adjustment more seriously than he. Yet he wondered how she could be so moody and so withdrawn at such an exciting time. Not knowing what else to do, he redoubled his tone of good cheer. On one occasion, he tried to get her to talk to him about her concerns, but she fell apart and ran off in tears. As a result, he gave up talking too personally to her and talked about their baby-to-be. It seemed the perfect way to avoid deeper issues.

&❧ *Jim is typical of most men who are not likely to face the reality of their new role in an open or conscious way. Protecting Carla is one way Jim has to avoid his own feelings. If he allows himself the luxury of dreaming about his new role, he might become aware of his own wishes to nurture and father his baby. He would have to face his feelings about his own father and about how much he will want to identify with him and relive his childhood experiences. He may not want to reproduce that relationship at all, but he, too, like Carla, must fall back on it as his most vital experience in preparation for this kind of role.*

In addition, a father's fears of a damaged infant often parallel those of his wife, although they may not be as intensely personal. Until recently, most men have suppressed these feelings. But fathers need to prepare themselves for a more sharing role with their wives, to venture into the "work" of attachment. They need to let their fears, ambivalences, and dreams come to the surface, to free up the energy they will need for attaching to the baby. It isn't easy for men to do this because sex stereotyping, though subtle, is still a fact of life.

Few of us had fathers who took part in our childhood care. They must carve out for themselves new territories. In the past, men adjusted only in a vicarious way, through their wives' readjustment. It avoided the possessiveness and competition for the baby that a more active attachment brings. Now we ask fathers to assume a more active, demanding role in the new family.

These days it is critical for men to prepare for their new family. Childbirth classes that include fathers-to-be are an enormous help in this. Fathers come to see me before the baby is born, hungrily looking for permission to consider themselves real participants. Clearly, it is time now to rid ourselves of the stereotype of the noninvolved male. I encourage fathers to go with their wives to obstetrical visits, and to take part in all the decisions about delivery and the new family. A man needs to adjust early to his new role. Jim's competition with Carla shows how involved he will be.

Whenever he called home, Jim was exuberant. He felt he was equal to his brothers now. He had a wife *and* a child. He pictured himself with a little girl who adored him, one who looked like a combination of Carla and a picture-book baby. And if it were a boy! He could teach him sports; he could do things with him every day. It would be his own baby—truly an amazing prospect!

On one occasion it dawned on Jim that he was becoming much too possessive and irritating to Carla. Once she had asked for a glass of wine. He had bristled and, before he realized it, said, "I don't think you should! You might hurt the baby." He stopped himself just in time from saying, " . . . my baby." After he said it, he realized how his remark must have sounded to Carla, and he tried valiantly to make it up to her. She seemed so vulnerable. He hadn't really been aware until that moment that this pregnancy might be coming between them. She was becoming so moody and withdrawn. He was too euphoric and too possessive, and it was endangering their relationship.

So Jim began to work harder at the office. He began to reevaluate his future in light of becoming a family man. Now he knew he must get ahead—and fast. So much depended on it. He understood why others at the office stayed later, worked harder, and played up to the boss, all the things he had deplored in the past. He always swore he would never become a workaholic, which was how he remembered his father, but he could understand it now. He justified his longer hours to Carla: "You won't be working for a while after the baby comes, so I have to work twice as hard now." She assured him coolly that the baby would not interfere with her work and he needn't worry about that.

It was getting harder for him to go along with her desire to return to work after the baby came. It seemed important to visualize her at home, in charge of "his" house and "his" baby. This was an unexpected turn in his thinking. Was he reverting to some old-fashioned fantasy, or to his own childhood? Perhaps he needed to think of himself as the all-powerful male with a barefoot woman in the house. Perhaps he was just identifying with "his" baby; and wishing for an ideal mother. Maybe his competition for the baby was driving him to press Carla into this single role.

* *A husband has a difficult time accepting his wife's new role. He projects onto her the struggle he is going through. Jim is really wishing that he could be home with the baby.*

Amniocentesis

Then came the next decision, amniocentesis. If they found out the baby was not right, would they have the courage to abort it? It seemed easier to ignore the possibility of a defect—and just pray. But they could not take responsibility for skipping this precaution, and their physician pressed them to do it: "It's a simple procedure. There's little risk." It didn't seem simple at all to Carla. To be invaded by a machine was bad enough, but to visualize the little squirming mass that was her baby made it even less possible to give it up. It was a pretty odd little thing, hardly a human being at all, but it was theirs, and it made the reality more credible. When faced with the question, "Do you want to know the sex?" they said they had already decided not to know.

    ❧ *Many couples today want to know the sex of the baby in advance, but many do not. Amniocentesis and even ultrasound can determine this. But Carla and Jim wanted a surprise, "like Christmas" and asked not to be told the sex in advance. This decision is a personal one. Each couple feels differently about it. Dr. Elizabeth Keller found that knowing the sex in advance did not speed up the attachment process to the baby after it arrived. Most parents feel they can adjust to either sex rather quickly, as long as the baby is intact.*

    However, amniocentesis has become almost routine to pregnant women over thirty-five, to discover any possible defects in the fetus. The fetus is located by ultrasound so that a needle can be safely inserted in the amniotic fluid sac, drawing off a few free-floating cells from the fluid to test. Relatively few defects show up in each fetal cell. The defects that can be identified are severe and well worth considering as a reason for abortion. They mean that the fetus will be a severely handicapped baby. The drawback of the test is that it is terribly difficult for parents to visualize the moving fetus and then have to consider the prospect of abortion. Newer tests, such as chorionic villous sampling, which means examining a bit of the placenta, can be done earlier and make the abortion decision, if necessary, somewhat easier. Every parent-to-be dreams of defects that might occur.

This anxiety is natural during pregnancy. Not only does this anxiety stir up energy, but, if the fetus is defective, these fantasies during pregnancy help prepare for the work of rehabilitation that will have to be done.

The test took two interminably long weeks. Finally, it was returned as normal, and they dared think of the baby as their own again. They began to wait for the fetal movement, which can be expected at five months.

Reactions of Others

The pregnancy remained full of both excitement and anxiety. But these feelings were not unique to Carla and Jim, and they found that they were joining a whole new community of parents. People they hardly knew became important to them all of a sudden, simply because they were parents. Their old crowd, still childless, began to shun them, as if they were contagious.

At the office, responses varied. Carla's boss began taking long-term assignments away from her, saying, "You won't be here long enough to do this." Or, "It wouldn't be fair to new clients to let them get used to you and then have you desert them." Some of the older partners implied that their ominous predictions about hiring unpredictable females had been fulfilled. Her younger male colleagues seemed smugly triumphant at the prospect of surviving her. A young woman colleague was both intrigued and awed by her "courage." None of these reactions bothered Carla as much as she had expected they would, because she herself was in a pink glow of excitement. She began to feel superior to most of the world around her, like the goose carrying the golden egg.

Quickening

When the fetus was five months old, Carla began to feel in her uterus a definite kind of movement. At first she thought it was a flutter of intestinal gas. Concentrating on a client one day, her mind began to wander. She couldn't quite place the strange feeling in her abdomen. It was like the breast of a bird held in one's hand. She stopped right in the middle of a very wise statement to place her hand on her lower belly. Then she smiled—benignly, with a faraway look in her eyes. It was the "quickening" or first movement of the fetus that she had read so much about. Her client seemed puzzled. She realized what she had done, blushed, and stammered, "I'm sorry, but I just felt my baby move. I'm pregnant, you know." Her client, a tough-minded business executive, said, "I'm sorry." She felt as if she had lost rapport with him and wondered whether she should turn him over to one of her colleagues. Instead, she tried to explain. "This is the first time I . . . ." She realized she was spending valuable business time talking about herself. It was embarrassing. However, the executive began to melt, and soon they were talking about *his* family. Before long they were in an animated personal conversation and she realized that their relationship had intensified. She returned to her advisory position with a whole new interest. When he left, she had her secretary call Jim's office with an "urgent message." She got him out of a conference to tell him the news. He whooped with delight. He asked how early she could get off, so he could "feel it, too." Actually, it would take another month before he could feel the movements. Meanwhile, they became more definite and predictable, occurring at certain times of the day. When Carla was busy, the baby was quiet. When she sat down at night, the baby moved. After a month she and Jim could share its movements. This made the pregnancy go faster.

As the baby began to move more and more, it became more of a reality for both of them. The thrill of feeling it move began to overcome all of the other conflicted feelings that had been bothering Carla. She now dared to believe it really *was* a baby and she really *was* a mother. The next few months were glorious. She felt well again, full of energy. She and Jim began to get close again. All the turmoil they had been through separately now seemed to cement them more closely together.

Their sexual relations were not easy any longer, however. Jim's desire wavered. He almost seemed to want to be in Carla's abdomen with the baby, yet dared not penetrate her for fear of hurting it. She, too, was torn. At times she wanted to be reassured that she was still desirable; at other times she just wanted to be left alone with "her" baby. She, too, was unreasonably afraid that intercourse might dislodge or damage the fetus. Her doctor tried to assure her that her fears were unreasonable, but there they were, and they made her cool and distant when Jim wanted her.

Daydreams

In this period, they began to feel an urgency to get on with their planning. They had wanted to move to a bigger apartment, but gave up on that in the first few months. Feverish looking replaced their inactivity. When they found one, but it was too expensive, they felt completely let down. They only wanted the best for the baby. They both realized they had to compromise more than ever before, if they were to make it with three mouths to feed on one salary. It wasn't likely, but they couldn't help thinking of Carla's job as potentially at risk. Carla didn't dare to go and see her boss; unconsciously she feared he would fire her.

When she dreamed of holding her baby, she could only think of herself as a mother. She dreamt of possibly giving up her job for a year or more so that she could be at home. She and Jim knew this was impossible, and so she never mentioned it, even though it was on both their minds. Perhaps they both felt that expressing the wish was too dangerously close to living it out.

&. *This fantasy of being the complete supermother is a kind of preparation for the role. It is a natural reaction and one to be indulged in. They both can wish for her to be an "at home mother" and at the same time realize that she must work. If they face it and discuss it, they can agree on the roles each will take, how long Carla can afford to be home, and so forth.*

As a result of warding off thoughts about returning to work, Carla began to try to detach herself from caring "too much" about the baby. In a recurrent dream she left the baby untended at home while she dashed off to work. She tried to reassure herself during the day that going off to work would not be a problem. But it already felt painful, and she was afraid to let her fantasies of mothering get out of control. She was already preparing for separation, long before the baby came.

As her pregnancy neared its end, Carla found it harder and harder to concentrate on her work. Her cases began to seem unimportant. She daydreamed about her baby and about herself as a mother, and worried about the quality of her work at the office.

  This last part of pregnancy is a critical time. This is when a woman gets ready emotionally to become a mother. The more Carla can sort things out ahead of time, the better prepared she will be to take on a new demanding role. She needs time to herself, to become wife and mother before the fact.

"Three Months at Half Pay"

Carla had originally planned to work right up until the end of her pregnancy, but she found that as the time grew nearer, she wasn't as productive as before. She wanted to be home making a nest for her baby. Weekends weren't long enough to paint the baby's room, to buy clothes and sort out hand-me-downs, to look at her and Jim's baby pictures, and just to dream. She was terribly relieved, though a bit threatened, when her boss suggested that she take the last few weeks off. Jokingly, he said, "It's hard for any of us—your colleagues or your clients—to concentrate on anything but your enormous belly." She knew he sensed how torn she was.

"How long can I stay away without losing all my clients?" Carla asked. Neither she nor her boss had faced the fact that she might want to stay home for a while after the baby came.

"Why don't you take three months off—at half pay. We can get along without you for that time," he said in his most generous manner.

Carla was both relieved and stunned. Relieved that it was out in the open at last. Stunned at the thought that three months at half pay seemed so finite. She could be a full-time mother at half pay for three whole months! All sorts of mixed feelings flooded over her at once—relief, joy in anticipation, the letdown of being sent away from her job, the reality of living on less than her whole salary. But the freedom she felt in being able to devote herself entirely to her new role overshadowed all the rest.

   ▲ Actually, three months at half pay is almost a put-down. Carla will find that this is not enough time to be at home with her baby. "Half pay" signifies the secondary role to which women "who are foolish enough to get pregnant" are assigned. We need to legislate the option for women to stay at home with a new baby on full subsidy. As a nation we can't afford to devalue motherhood in such a way. As long as it is left to individual firms to decide, their own needs will come first and mothering second. At such a time women deserve both real and symbolic support.

Preparation

Carla set to work feverishly to "fill up her days." She cleaned the baby's room several times. She washed all the new baby clothes; she sorted out piles of hand-me-downs. She read all she could on how to mother her baby. Jim came home early each night, wanting to join in her excitement and anticipation. He, too, spent most of his days with only half his mind on his work. He dreamt of the little boy he could toss in the air; the little girl he could show off.

   ▲ We Americans are still immersed in sex stereotyping. No matter how sincerely we plan to treat the sexes alike, we usually have very different expectations for, and behave very differently with, each sex. Few fathers dream of throwing a girl baby around, nor do they expect to cuddle a boy baby in the same gentle way. If we want to raise boys and girls alike, it won't be easy. Such a change comes slowly.
   Fathers need to be able to take leave from their work, too. We should take seriously what many other nations (Sweden, Russia, and Denmark, to name a few) are already doing. In Chapter 4, I offer suggestions for a national policy.

The Last Month

So far Carla's pregnancy had been a normal one. Yet they dreaded as well as looked forward to the next step. In the last month, they had attended childbirth classes together. The classes were exciting, rewardingly on the mark, and they waited eagerly for each one. All the other couples felt the same combination of euphoric anticipation and dread. It helped to share their feelings about labor and birth, earlier experiences, childcare, and their two careers. Carla and Jim felt surrounded with goodwill. Their helpless feelings were shared by the others, and this in itself reassured them. They listened to the other couples' trials in adjustment and began to see that the work they had done together had been worthwhile. By the time labor began, they knew they'd make it.

A Real Baby

As Carla entered labor, both she and Jim were ready. Jim helped Carla through her labor pains right up to the end, and Carla felt like the original earth mother—so easy was the delivery. A lusty, alert baby girl looked them each in the eye as if to say, "Well, here I am. Let's get going."

So perfect was this new creature, so self-assured, that Carla and Jim felt as if they had always known her. She was solid to feel; she moved gracefully; she cried to be fed; she looked at their faces and listened to their voices as if she knew exactly what they were saying to her. They called her "Amy" because she was so like Carla's sister, Amelia. Amy made becoming a parent easy. Not only were they enraptured with her, but they felt grateful to her. Every signal from her seemed clear. Every response seemed reasonable.

The First Few Weeks

Carla's mother came to help them out during their first week at home. She had taken part of her vacation time to be with them, and they were grateful, but they didn't really need her. Amy was so easy to care for.

    ❧ *New mothers tell me that one of the problems in being able to turn to their own mothers at such a time is that most grandmothers are now working, too. In order to be available to help with a new baby, they must leave their jobs. Few grandparents are nearby or available for babysitting when new mothers return to work. These days, the extended family is often not available as a cushion for new young parents. Carla and Jim are luckier than most. To have a caring, supportive grandparent is the best start any couple can have. Even if you don't agree with what she says and does, it gives you a sounding board and options to think about. It is much harder to have no ideas at all and to have to find your way alone.*

The first three weeks were easier than any of them had anticipated. Carla said she felt like a real mother. Jim said this was what he'd wanted all his life. He held Amy constantly when he was at home. When he had to go to work, he could hardly stand to leave her and came back several times for a "last goodbye." When she whimpered, they both jumped to see what was wrong.

    ❧ *Parents always ask me whether or not it is possible to spoil a new baby. When we pursue it, what they seem to mean is that by holding the baby they may get her too "used to being held," and when they put her down, "she will cry." I think all babies need to be held, and their parents need the joy of holding them. The closeness that the parent and infant feel becomes a secure base on which a sense of trust in each other is built. Holding and being close to a baby is not likely to spoil her. On the other hand, if a parent feels trapped or unable to separate from the baby, the baby will sense the parent's ambivalence very quickly. The tension will cause the baby to be tense. She will cry, and the parent will feel guilty and torn and will jump to quiet her. More tension will build between them, and the baby will become anxious and fretful. This is where the spoiling comes from, not from the mutually rewarding experience of holding and being held. It is in the baby's best interest as well as your own to examine your feelings and deal openly with them. At a certain point, not being held by an ambivalent, angry parent may be better for the baby than being held or carried.*

Breast-Feeding

Carla desperately wanted to breast-feed Amy, and discussed it with Dr. Jones, Amy's new doctor. He assured Carla that it would be worth it to start out and see how it went. He was pretty sure she could manage to keep her milk going longer than three months, when she would be returning to work. They could fall back on a bottle of formula for Amy during the day. If Carla learned to use a breast pump, she might even be able to leave her own milk frozen for Amy while she was gone. In any case, Dr. Jones assured Carla that it was certainly worth it to start out on the breast. They could always wean Amy in a week's time, if necessary.

ଈ The closeness that comes with successful breast-feeding is a mother's major reward. And, for a working mother away part of the day, the opportunity to enhance this closeness by nursing the baby at the end of the working day is a real plus. I think breast-feeding is of extra importance to a working mother in maintaining the attachment between her and her baby. Some firms—and I wish there were more—have day-care centers or substitute care nearby so that mothers can get to their babies to breast-feed them, at lunch and at coffee breaks. The industries that try this find that the mothers' productivity increases dramatically. The allegiance a mother feels for a firm that "nurtures" her in this way outweighs any other "reward" the firm could provide her.

Carla and Jim had been warned that Amy might get set against taking milk from a bottle unless they started her on a nipple early. Indeed, when they tried her on a bottle at ten days old, she shut her mouth firmly and turned her head away from it into Carla's breast. In dismay, Carla thought, she doesn't want anyone but me. If I didn't have to go back to work so soon, I could feed her all by myself. However, Amy proved willing to take the bottle from Jim, but only if Carla was out of the room. If she heard or sensed Carla's presence, she refused.

❧ Carla may be already beginning to anticipate the separation down the road. Every step toward leaving Amy will be especially difficult while the process of attachment is still so strong. I wonder how a mother who knows she must leave her baby in the first few weeks can ever allow herself to attach wholeheartedly to that baby. It is too painful to recognize the delicious closeness, only to give it up.

A Fussy Baby

The end of the honeymoon came when Amy was eighteen days old. Until then, she had seemed so good. She did nothing but eat and sleep on an increasingly predictable schedule. Carla's milk had been plentiful, and Amy was efficient in taking it. She had slept most of the time in between feedings and, when she woke up, was pleasant, looking around patiently while they changed her. Carla had called her mother and said, "If I'd known it was this easy and this delightful, I'd have started having babies years ago!"

Then one evening Amy started fussing. They both leapt to her side to find out what was wrong. They changed her diapers. They fed her. They burped her. They rocked her. Still she fussed. Each new attention seemed to quiet her for a moment, but as they continued to try out one thing after another, she became more frantic. Carla cried and Jim paced frantically back and forth. Finally, they each called their mothers, in preparation for taking Amy to the hospital. Each grandmother suggested a series of things they'd already tried. Each wondered what Carla had eaten to "ruin her milk." Carla had become so distraught that she felt no milk at all in her breasts. When she tried Amy on the bottle or breast, the baby sucked once or twice, then turned her head as if in utter despair.

Carla felt thoroughly rejected, at a loss. They called Dr. Jones, sure that he would send them off to the hospital. Amy's doctor listened patiently, then said quietly, "I'm afraid she's just getting into a normal crying period. It will probably happen every day now until she's three months old. Nothing is wrong with her. Nothing you do will calm her down entirely. This is a normal part of a small baby's day and it won't hurt her to cry. But it will be hard for you. Try each thing you know to do. Feed her, change her, comfort her, carry her. Be sure she's not in any pain that you can recognize. If nothing works, don't worry too much. Babies *do* cry at the end of every day—just to let off steam. She'll do better if you don't overstimulate her, so put her down, let her cry for fifteen or twenty minutes, pick her up, put her down again, until she's finally let off enough energy. You'll find she's better organized after such a period. She'll sleep and eat better the rest of the day. Babies sort of 'disintegrate' after an overstimulating day."

This was very reassuring. Dr. Jones sounded so sure of himself that Carla and Jim began to relax. Amy stopped fussing and went off to sleep. The crisis had passed, and Carla and Jim felt like they had been through their first real trauma. Could they stand another? Sometimes Carla wanted to run out of the house. Jim wished he could go back to work. Neither of them dared to face how really upset Amy's crying had made them.

&. *Dr. Constance Keefer, a pediatrician in my unit, did a prospective study with some professional women who were about to become mothers for the first time. They all had important jobs to which they needed to return as soon as possible. They all felt torn by their desire to be "at home" with this first baby. Their predictions about when they thought they would return to work were not matched later by the reality of when they actually did go back. Instead, their return to work correlated more with the kind of baby they had. If the baby was difficult, inconsolable and unpredictable, the mother returned to work earlier than predicted. If, on the other hand, the baby was easy, predictable, and rewarding, the mother found excuses not to return on time.*

My concern is for mothers who leave before they have learned to deal with this fussiness. If they go back to work at this time and leave the baby to another's care, they are likely to continue to feel helpless and inadequate about any future crying episode.

It is the nature of a small baby to "fall apart" this way. If parents can learn to tolerate it they can continue to feel that they are still in control. Learning to deal with negative behaviors is as critical as learning about the baby's smiles and other positive behaviors. A new mother should not leave her baby before she masters this. Hence, the first four months should be inviolate. Many babies have three months of crying, or colic, at the end of the day. A new mother needs to realize that it's not her fault and that they can survive together for three months and even learn to love each other later—by the fourth month.

A fussy period is, as Dr. Jones said, common in babies of this age. From three to twelve weeks, crying at the end of the day is predictable. Although these periods shake up the parents' self-confidence, they also contribute to the intensity of the parents' relationship. When parents finally accept the fact that there is no "right" way to meet every occurrence, when they see the baby survive such a nighmarish experience, they begin to believe in the inner strength of the baby. When they live through ten weeks of fussing, and the baby continues to flourish, they become less anxious. When it finally comes to an end, they feel as if they were really on their way. New parents need to get through this period of intense adjustment and enjoy the feeling of having "lived through it" together.

Competition

Carla began to worry more and more about leaving Amy. She realized that her three-months' leave would end when Amy was only ten weeks old. Each day became precious to her. Each day Amy achieved something new. Carla could see how hard it was for Jim to leave Amy each day. Each day he called home to tell Carla he had made it to work okay. He had never done that before. Carla knew he just wanted to hear about Amy, and she began saying things like, "Amy and I miss you already." "How do you know she does?" "Amy looks around as if she expected more than my voice and my face." Jim giggled appreciatively. He called home at lunch and again at five o'clock. Carla realizes how much he loved having his "little family" at the other end of the phone. He was keeping tabs on her.

➣ *Being at home with a small baby must be completely satisfying at times. But it must as well be oppressive for someone as active as Carla. Carla may long for Jim's kind of freedom to come and go, while he may long to stay at home and be close to Amy. Many young women say they feel "trapped" when they are at home alone with a small baby. We should consider how lonely a job mothering can be. Isolated new mothers need support from other mothers who are in the same stage of contemplating separating from their babies to return to work. To leave or not to leave can be a very painful decision.*

Every night Jim rushed past Carla at the door and headed straight for Amy's room. Carla experienced some of her old feelings of resentment. She was being overlooked. She would say things like, "Jim, don't wake her up. I just got her fed and put away." Or "Remember this is when she always starts fussing— maybe it's because you overstimulate her." As soon as she said it she felt foolish. She was being so territorial about Amy. She really wanted Jim to share the joy as well as the work, but she couldn't help feeling that her closeness with Amy was being invaded. And time was getting short. Soon she would have to give Amy up to someone else.

➣ *The competition all parents feel over a new baby came as a real surprise to Carla and Jim. If they let them, these feelings could come between them. But if they see these feelings as part of their developing closeness to Amy, they can grow closer to each other.*

Reprieve

At eight weeks, when Amy began to smile at Carla in a predictable way every time she spoke to her, Carla made up her mind. She just couldn't leave her in anyone else's care yet. One more month seemed too short. It was right around the corner. Would another woman know what to do if Amy cried? Would she know how to hold her in a certain way so that Amy would feel "at home"? Would she be patient when Amy refused the bottle?

Carla found herself weeping during the day whenever she thought about it. She tried to discuss it with Jim at night. At first he was sympathetic. He said he knew it would be hard for her. Then he began to try to cheer her up. He also warned her about losing her job; he reminded her of how far she'd come. It all fell on deaf ears, and he got impatient. He was angry that she might not be ready to separate at the agreed-upon time.

     🍂 *Carla's struggle is reviving Jim's own difficulty in separating. As he argues about her problems in leaving Amy, he's really talking to himself, although he cannot yet admit to it. Their feelings of competition and territoriality are still pretty raw.*

Carla made up her own mind and called her office. She told her boss she couldn't come back in four weeks when the agreed-upon three-months leave would be up. The silence was interminable. She feared he might just say that she needn't return at all. But she had been determined enough to risk it, and he sensed it. He said, "Carla, we want you back. We all miss your good sense and your wisdom. When will you be ready?" She asked him whether she could start part time, leaving the baby for only a four-hour stint initially. He grumblingly agreed, and she offered to begin when Amy was four months old—another precious month at home!

     🍂 *This fourth month, in my opinion, will be solid gold for both Carla and Amy. However, we need to know more than we do about ages at which babies can be left. We need to know what developmental processes may be at risk in a shared caretaking situation. At what age can an infant master three important relationships? In extended family cultures, babies are handed from one member to another, but the style of caregiving is so similar that there is no real disruption for the baby. In long-term follow-up studies of babies who have been in day-care situations in infancy, many researchers find that there is no recognizable difference in later intellectual or emotional development. There are too few carefully documented studies to reassure parents who must leave their small children in secondary care.*

The most important thing to remember is that a small baby should be left in the care of someone who has the time and the energy to care about her, to respond when she smiles or vocalizes, to let her know that that was an important and exciting thing to have done. Without a responsive person, each new accomplishment will become less rewarding to her and she will lag in her development. Babies who are severely deprived can fail to grow and gain weight, unable to use calories even when they are provided. This kind of deprivation is fortunately rare, but it is devastating.

Look first for a warm, caring person. Then be sure that that person is not overloaded with responsibilities. For instance, in day-care, there should be no more than three small babies per adult. In larger centers, there are enough adults for flexible exchanges. There a ratio of four infants to one adult may be permissible, but the adults should be well trained. These are critical months for a baby's development. No wonder Carla worries about going back to work!

2

The Thompsons

When Alice Thompson came to my office, I made the mistake of asking for her spouse's name. "I'm not married." she said. When I asked her whether the father of her baby would be participating with her in its delivery, she answered curtly, "No!" I realized that she was not letting me in on her situation, and so I pursued it. "Will he be of any support with the new baby?" At this, she exploded, "I came to you because one of my friends told me you helped her with being a single parent. I've made a conscious and careful choice. I want a baby but I don't want a husband. So I'm not just some poor pregnant girl who got abandoned. Just the contrary. I deserted *him* after he helped me do what I wanted."

I told her gently that I thought she was being a little defensive and that she needn't be with me. I'd been through this with other women and respected them for their clear decision. However, I had to be honest with her, I said, and point out that it isn't always easy to be a single parent. The reality isn't likely to be as romantic as the dream. "Unless we understand and trust each other, I can never be of the kind of help you need." She said, "I don't need help." "Maybe you're misunderstanding what

27

I mean by help," I replied, "You'll need the support and advice that an outside person can give you. It's a hard job to raise a baby alone."

"Are you trying to scare me? This is something I've thought about for a long, long time. I'm over thirty, and I'm ready to settle down." Indeed she did look determined. Her chin jutted out as she spoke, and her eyes filled with the strength of her feelings. Her presence was admirable, and I wanted to reach out to her.

"I only want to be as much of a participant as you want me to be, but in order to do that I need to understand as much about your circumstances as I can." She softened, sat slightly back in the chair, and began to tell me more about herself. She was a sculptress, she told me. Lately she had been living off her art and some teaching. She had mastered the technique she was after and had found a following. Now she wanted to fulfill another side of her life. Her parents were an hour away; and they had been told of her decision. They didn't agree with it, but they would help her if she needed it. She'd had one serious attachment years ago. No other man since appealed to her as a husband, and she knew that people could and were raising children alone. She wanted her baby. She was determined to do whatever she needed to do to make it work. She knew she could be a good mother. As she talked, she leaned forward again. Her earnestness and her need to do a good job by this baby came through. I liked her already and knew we could work together.

꙰ The number of single-parent families is increasing rapidly. Most are the result of a high divorce rate and of teenage out-of-wedlock pregnancies, but many are deliberately planned. More often now, unmarried women come to my office, declaring that they never intended to have a husband. They want a baby, but not the added responsibility of a spouse.

A significant number of husbands and wives leave their spouses when a new baby adds an extra burden to a marriage. The tenuous balance the couple had achieved doesn't work any more with a baby between them. Jealously and feelings of inadequacy arise around the baby, and the less-committed parent leaves home.

In all these situations the remaining parent needs extra support and understanding to cope with the predictable difficulties in the job of raising a small infant. A single parent is usually a working parent as well; hence, all of the issues I raised in the last chapter are also faced by single parents, and are more intense.

I then explained to Alice how I saw my role, partly to reassure her, partly to seal our contract. "I do understand now, and I can be of help to you, if you'll let me. I've found that single parents need at least two kinds of support. One is simply guidance pointing out where you've come from and where you're going. That's pretty universal for the parents I've met in my practice. You need some idea of what the developmental issues for your baby are and will be in the near future. The other kind of support is more critical for a single parent. You will need me to help you with decisions about discipline because you will be the sole disciplinarian. And you will need advice and urging to let the baby go. That is the hardest job of being a single parent. Your own need to hang on to the baby for yourself, your fear of the unknown, will very likely cloud your vision when it comes time to consider your baby's need for independence. You'll need me to point this out. It won't be easy, and I know that. But it will be critical to let your baby go when he or she is ready. You don't want a child who is tied to your apron strings, or one who feels incompetent as a person, I know."

She nodded seriously, as if she'd become aware of this already. Then she whispered softly, "I almost don't want to let this baby deliver: I feel so fulfilled now with him—or her—inside of me." At this, she blushed. I knew, by this admission, that we were now on the same wavelength.

Support

I asked her who would be with her during labor and delivery. Were her parents involved? Would they be here for the big event? Though they lived close by, she said she hadn't thought of asking her mother to come and be with her. As I asked, I could see that

Alice was already thinking about it more deeply. I quoted a study in the *New England Journal of Medicine* by Drs. John Kennell and Marshall Klaus in which they found that having a *doula*, or attendant, at childbirth significantly changed the outcome of delivery—the amount of drugs and anesthesia necessary, the duration of labor, and the number of cesarean sections were all statistically lower. The mother's attitude about herself and her baby seemed to be affected also. Supportive companionship in labor gave the mother more confidence in herself—a critical factor in passing self-confidence on to the baby later on.

Alice said, "I think I'll ask my mother. If I knew she'd come, I might try the childbirth education classes. I haven't really dared to go to them. Everyone there is in couples, and I would feel uncomfortable."

    What Alice said is true. Childbirth classes are busy soliciting fathers' participation. They have been so successful that most participants have their spouses with them. There are still no prenatal classes for single parents-to-be.

I wondered, and asked Alice, whether she thought this reflected an underlying feeling that to be alone in childbirth and childrearing is a bit frightening and second-rate. She asserted bravely that she tried to put this out of her mind, but she guessed it really did. After that, we talked more freely about how she would face this lingering feeling in the future. How would she handle her own and her baby's—feelings about being an "incomplete" family?

    I am convinced that questions from children about why they or their families are different must be handled right from the start. Not before children are ready but when the questions come from them voluntarily. If the parent faces up to her side of it, she will be ready to say, "This is the way we are. Every family is different and has something special to live with. In our case, it's that we don't have a daddy. We do have a grandma and grandpa, and maybe someday we'll get a daddy. But you and I love each other and that's our family." Facing it for herself ahead of time will give Alice the strength and conviction she needs to

*carry it off without apology, without being defensive. Children
need such a strong, firm conviction as backup in dealing with
their peers and their own self-image.*

Alice did call her mother, who was very moved and said she
would come for the delivery, but couldn't come to the childbirth
classes. Alice braved these out alone and—when the time
came—prepared herself for the delivery. Her mother came and
sat with her and her labor and delivery went well, with no medication and only local anesthesia. Her baby girl was a healthy
seven-and-a-half pounds. When I went in to see Alice, both she
and the baby were wide awake and looking at each other in
absolute awe. The baby's grandmother sat peacefully in the corner of the room, watching her daughter with admiration. I had
difficulty extracting the baby from Alice's arms, so I examined
her right there on her mother's abdomen. The baby was perfect
physically, and I said so with complete assurance. Alice sighed.
"I was so afraid she'd be marked, or that I might have damaged
her by my own impetuousness. I really shouldn't have dared to
bring such a perfect little being into such an imperfect setup."
She looked at me pleadingly for reassurance.

I looked at her squarely. "Alice," I said, "you made up your
mind to do this in good faith. Of course you have doubts now,
but you have to face them for *her* sake, so you can be as strong
for her as she needs you to be." I turned to Alice's mother and
said, "The fact that you and her father are behind her is a real
source of strength for all of us. I hope you'll stay in the picture."
Her mother said fervently, "We want this baby as much as Alice
does, and we'll see to it that she knows she has us." I knew this
would be a real plus for the future of Alice and her baby, Tina.

&.* Alice's fears and feelings of incompleteness are naturally high at such a critical time. They will be again at every
real crisis in Tina's life. No matter how thoroughly Alice has
faced her own questions about whether this was the right thing
to have done, doubts about the wisdom of flying in the face of
custom will arise each time she copes with a new crisis. Each
time, she will ask herself, Have I done this baby any harm by
bringing her into an "incomplete" family? Am I good enough?
These are inevitable questions for single parents. They ask them*

because they care. The support of grandparents is very impor-
tant in the face of these doubts.

As I examined Tina, I brought out some of the infant's exciting responses: her ability to turn toward my voice; to look at and follow my face; to calm herself down by getting her fist up to her own mouth when she was upset; to choose her mother's voice over mine as we talked to her from different directions. As we watched her, her mother and her grandmother both said, "Why, she's already a person!"

➤ *It's vital to let Alice see that Tina already has a person-ality and strengths all her own. I will have to help Alice keep this fact uppermost. It's too easy for doting adults to submerge, or "spoil," a baby. Tina is likely to need all the ego strength she can muster to develop her own independence.*

Over the next few days, Alice's breast milk came in, and Tina successfully adjusted to breast-feeding. I urged Alice to stay in the hospital an extra day—to be sure she got her milk estab-lished, and to gather all the information and support she could from the nurses before she left.

➤ *Feeling secure and supported is critical to breast-feed-ing, especially for a first-time mother. Being at home alone with a new baby always produces anxiety, no matter what the cir-cumstances. If Alice's mother can be there as a source of support without judging Alice, she can help a lot. But I wasn't sure that I wanted to test this. A hospital is not necessarily the most positive environment, but Alice knows that the nursing staff there will support her and that they know how to help her get the feedings going. An extra day can be a good investment.*

At home, Alice had a hard time of it. Not with Tina, for the baby was an alert, responsive, active baby. But Alice began to feel depressed, full of self-doubts. She needed to call me almost daily.

&* *I expect this with most new mothers, but especially with single parents. The inevitable postpartum blues loom larger and seem more insurmountable. Self-doubts are harder to allay. The need for a spouse is never so great as in a crisis. This is true even when the spouse is falling apart, too. The old saying holds—"Misery loves company."*

I urged Alice to call each morning until she felt more secure. I urged her as well to let her mother stay nearby and be of help. "But my mother and I are getting on each other's nerves. She doesn't trust anything I do, and I feel her criticism everytime I turn around." I tried to point out that maybe these were natural feelings as she tried to find her own ways of doing things for Tina. I told her I was sure that her mother's being there was a support. It was worth it to have someone with whom she could give vent to her feelings and thoughts.

After ten days, Alice was more confident, and her mother was ready to go back to her own home. Alice's self-questioning had subsided, and she seemed to be more self-reliant. Now she called me only twice a week. I suggested that she join a parent group which had been formed by the maternity nurses. All the new parents in it were in the same stage that Alice was in. They all needed each other, and could learn from each other in a supportive environment. Alice hesitated because no one in the group was single. I pushed her to go anyway, and it worked like a charm. Alice developed several close friends. They admired each other's babies and spent hours together on the phone.

&* *Childbirth education groups have shown many parents the way. There is nothing quite so supportive and informative as a group of peers all trying to achieve similar goals. There are many benefits for Alice. The group helps her fight against her terrible loneliness and exposes her to a lot of new ideas about childrearing. No matter how rewarding a new baby can be— and is—there is still a void without adult companionship at such a time.*

The loneliness even in two-parent nuclear families is all the more striking when one has seen in other cultures the effect of the extended family. All of the women in the family gather around the new mother to cosset and instruct her. That would be over-

powering to anyone from our culture—just as Alice's mother is for her. But lateral peer relationships are an enormous help at such a time. I recommend peer groups for all new, insecure mothers—and fathers! Men have a harder time forming and staying in a group—especially when they need each other. Daring to be close to each other is not easy for new fathers.

Predictable Fussing

Tina was the kind of active, intense baby who was bound to develop a fussy period at the end of each day. I knew this would be difficult for Alice to face, so I started preparing her for it early. I warned her that most alert, exciting babies seem to disintegrate at the end of the day. I hoped to soften the inevitable anxiety she would feel about Tina or about her handling of Tina.

     ❧ Understanding ahead of time something as painful as a baby crying can be very helpful for parents. They are less anxious and are able to listen. After crying spells begin, parents can't really hear a doctor's explanation. However, it wasn't until Tina began crying each day that Alice understood the significance of what I had said.

Tina fussed every evening, and, every morning Alice called me to be sure it was "really all right." Wasn't there something she could do to stop it? Her friends were trying special diets, gripe water, drugs—all seemed to help. Why wouldn't I help her find something? I reiterated my own conviction that this was part of Tina's day and was not likely to be helped by any of the crutches she described. Alice's anxiety and fussing over the baby would only reinforce the crying. She called me a week later to tell me I was right. None of her friends' remedies had really changed anything, and she was grateful that I pressed her to understand and to live with it.

     ❧ Alice is developing well as a mother. She deals with her anxiety in many mature ways—by relying on me, on her friends,

and on her own intelligence. She can take information, try it out, and discard it when it doesn't work.

After Tina was six weeks old, she began to sleep longer at night. She still cried predictably for an hour and a half each evening, but Alice had a routine now. She tended to her in any way she could, rocking her until that no longer helped. At that point, she would put her down for a fifteen-or twenty-minute period. She said she knew Tina's pattern now; she would build up to a short burst of wailing, then was ready to be picked up and played with. Next, after a joyful half hour of smiles and gurgles, she would disintegrate and Alice would put her back down. Following two or three more cycles of fussing and playing together, Alice rocked her baby. The rocking soothed Tina. Her heavy-lidded eyes and glazed stare told Alice that Tina was ready for a last little snack at the breast. After a short burst of sucks, Tina was almost asleep. Then, Alice would put her face down and tuck her in, crooning softly to her. Tina went off into a deep sleep. She would sleep for six hours afterward.

   Tina is sleeping longer at night at an early age. It's an excellent sign—of successful breast-feeding, of a maturing nervous system, and of Alice's ability to fit into Tina's pattern for fussiness and sleep.

Sharing a Baby

Tina began to smile and to vocalize, and Alice thought she'd burst with joy. She sat and watched Tina—awake or asleep—by the hour. She could barely stand to leave her at night, and often thought of taking her to bed with her. Somewhere in the back of her mind, though, she was afraid of such intense closeness. Tina began to smile, to chortle and laugh at her, and Alice felt rewarded. It was all for her. When she thought of calling her mother to tell her about it, she had a curious reaction—she really didn't want to share Tina's behavior. Her mother might want to come over to see these new developments, and her presence might dilute the meaning of Tina's behavior for Alice. Alice realized she didn't want to see Tina perform for anyone else. She wanted to believe that these reactions were for her alone. One day, while wheeling Tina in the park, an acquaintance came up to admire her baby. Tina brightened and smiled at the stranger. Alice felt a rush of jealousy. As she pulled Tina away from this "intruder," she realized she was becoming almost pathological about her relationship with Tina. She refused to go out on dates now. She asked no one over to dinner. She was becomming a recluse, indulging herself in a "love affair" with Tina.

Alice was amazed at the intensity of her reactions—and a bit frightened of them. For the first time in her adult life, she was completely and utterly in love. Each morning her heart raced as she thought of the day ahead—with Tina. To touch her soft cheeks, to cuddle her, to feed her at her own breast were all such wonderful experiences that she felt a pang of uneasiness each day. What price would she have to pay for this happiness? She had never experienced any pleasure that didn't have a price. This must have a big one.

All new parents feel this way, but most do not let them-selves get so carried away. This reaction may represent how lonely and isolated Alice had felt during pregnancy and in meet-ing this enormous responsibility alone. Being a single parent is surely not easy. But the rewards can be as great as Alice is finding them to be. It will be easier in the long run if Alice allows herself to share Tina more. Otherwise, the separation, which is bound to come as Tina develops more independence, will be-come more and more difficult. In one way, Alice has reason to feel uneasy. This kind of overpowering relationship will not be easy to dilute. Tina's goal is to establish her own independence. This is one of the most difficult aspects of a single parent's relationship with a child.

Leaving Tina to return to work became the most terrible thing Alice could imagine. Although she had worried about raising her baby alone she somehow now realized that it wasn't really a conscious decision. She had always wanted a baby for herself. Pregnancy and having the baby had fulfilled those wishes, which turned out to be more rewarding than she could ever have anticipated. It was as if she had climbed a tall mountain all by herself. Reaching the top had been more gratifying than she had believed.

Very soon Alice was able to elicit a smile from Tina whenever she wanted one. Vocalizations were harder to come by, but low-throated gurgles and coos began to appear by two months. She decided to call her mother and father to come see and hear all this. At first, they weren't able to get Tina to smile or coo. She looked hard at these strangers, with a frown on her face, as if to say, "Who are you?" After a while, Tina began to include them in her largesse. Both grandparents were hers after this. They offered to babysit or at least be on hand whenever Alice needed them. Tina had won them over.

&. *Alice ought to take them up on their offer to babysit, but she probably won't. Leaving a baby with someone else is even harder for a single parent than it is for a couple. The fear of something going wrong is always there, and, as attachment to the baby grows, so does this unnamed fear. Developing the habit of getting away a bit to do something fun would be wise for Alice. One of the most difficult things about being alone in the job of childrearing is to remember that recreation balances a life. The difficulty for Alice is that she knows so few in her same situation. With other couples, she feels she sticks out like a sore thumb. Very few single women, and even fewer single men, have children. So home feels like the most gratifying place to be.*

When Alice brought Tina to my office for the eight-week visit, I sensed the intensity of their relationship. I asked Alice about Tina, but she shared very little. Her responses were guarded. I pointed this out to her, and she clutched Tina a bit closer. I could barely see Tina's face, and asked Alice whether Tina was beginning to smile and vocalize. "Only at me." "Could I hold her to see whether she will smile at me?" Alice stiffened and pulled away, and I realized that she was having a problem sharing Tina. I felt Alice's protective tension mount as I tried to explore her relationships with other people.

&. *One difficult part of being a single parent is learning to share a baby, and to "let her go."*

I placed Tina on my examining table and leaned over her. Alice inserted herself between us, and I had to work around her to examine Tina. When I picked Tina up to weigh her, Alice put her hands up as if to catch Tina in case I dropped her. I sensed the intensity of Alice's feelings about Tina and decided we should begin to address them together.

     I could easily have gotten irritated with Alice at this point. This kind of overprotective symbiosis seemed almost pathological. It certainly didn't bode well for Tina's future. How could Alice let Tina achieve independence? How could she learn to share Tina? So far, she had never left Tina's side. Would Tina be a spoiled child? These questions ran through my mind. But I realized that this baby filled an enormous need in Alice. Tina was probably the first person who Alice felt was completely hers. I had to help Alice see that this deep caring relationship, although the most wonderful thing that could ever happen to Tina, would limit Tina's development. I knew that, if I didn't make my point, Alice might need to run away from me. I could do it if I handled her feelings with respect. Her smothering behavior was built on love, not on ambivalence.

I asked her a bit more about her past. Alice looked surprised. "What does that have to do with Tina's health? I don't want to be pried into!" I assured her I wasn't prying, but I had to play a very active role if I were to help her do the very best for Tina, and I knew that's what she wanted. At that point Alice said, "You know, it's funny. Since Tina was born, I don't really want anyone else in our lives, not even you. But I realize that I'm not thinking of Tina's future." I assured her that I could understand that kind of reaction and that my examination of Tina might seem intrusive. Tina smiled up at me from the examining table, and I remarked to Alice how delicious Tina's smiles and gurgles were. I also assured her that I did want to protect all of the feelings of attachment between the two of them. For they were critical to Tina's development. But I also knew how hard it would be in the future—for both of them—if Tina could not develop any independence, and so I would have to play the role of advocate for Tina's development. A single parent needs a more objective outsider to point out the child's developmental issues when they surface. If Tina is to develop a sense of herself as a person, Alice will need to learn to share her with others. To her credit, Alice heard what I was trying to say to her. "I knew the axe would fall. It was all too good to be true—having Tina all to myself."

We spent a few minutes exploring Alice's own past experiences—with her mother, her father, her brothers, and her relationship with Tina's father. We talked about her lonely childhood, a time when she had never really been cared for by others, when she felt all her relationships were one-sided. I could see then that Tina filled a need that Alice had never faced. As we talked, Alice began to relax a bit. "You know, I wasn't aware how all this might affect my relationship with Tina and how I handle her. Of course you need to know more about me—so you can help us both." I let Alice know how much I admired her for being able to unload all of this, and I assured her that I could help.

At this point, she seemed resigned. She said, "Well, what must I do?" I asked her why she felt she must do something. She answered, "I know you want me to start sharing Tina." I said I hoped she was sure enough of their relationship and of her own capacity as a good mother to be able to do so. "Why not get to know some other parents, maybe another single parent,—they'd have the same feelings and problems you do." She looked at me in disbelief. I pointed out to her that maybe her reaction to my suggestion reflected her own wish to be different from all other mothers (or her fear of being different). I gave her the name of two other single mothers I knew and suggested that she get in touch with them. By this time, she seemed almost giddy with relief, and I pointed this out to her. She didn't need to be so isolated. Both she and Tina would have a better time if they could share and be shared.

When time came to inoculate Tina for diphtheria, whooping cough and tetanus, Alice was ready to hold her for me. Rather than guard Tina from me, she could reassure her that I would not hurt her. Tina sensed her mother's reassuring tone, and as I inserted the needle, Alice winced. When they left, Alice was happier, more open, and I knew we had begun the process that is difficult for any new mother—realizing a child's need for her own identity.

Two weeks later, Alice called to tell me that she had been able to get together with the other mothers. She told me how much the babies had enjoyed it and how much each of the mothers had gotten out of discussing their problems with each other. In triumph she said, "Now I'm ready for my mother to babysit. I want to share Tina with her."

&. *We know much about the therapeutic value of support groups for* all *new parents. The Childbirth Education Groups, begun in Boston in 1957, are a powerful force in preparing women (and men) for their roles in natural childbirth without medication. They also effectively provide new, young parents a sense of not being alone. Even where the groups are not officially maintained after delivery, many isolated parents seek each other out to compare their experiences. It is an important way to share feelings, to learn about others' experiences, and to establish common values for their children's future. In Alice's case, it is particularly important. The other single mothers have the same difficulties with separation. They can share ideas and their anxiety and can help each other find solutions. Single parents need not feel so isolated these days, and it protects their infants' future if they don't. A feeling of communality, of knowing others, in the same situation, is critical to prevent a kind of narcissistic isolation in their children later on. When parents don't have to be defensive, they can allow their children to feel independent and at the same time feel that they are "like other children." The early months are the time to start that process.*

Steps Toward Independence

Tina needed more food than she was getting. Alice had intended to breast-feed her throughout the first year. But, at four months, Tina began to look around after a feeding as if she were still hungry. Alice's heart sank. Would feeding her solid food be the first wedge between them? I encouraged her to start, but to go slowly so that Tina would not miss more than one breast-feeding. Three or four feedings would keep Alice's milk coming.

&. *Many mothers are afraid that solid food will interfere with breast-feeding, and the fear itself—if great enough—can interfere with milk production. Solids, started slowly and judiciously, can supplement the breast milk.*

Every new step in Tina's development foretells her future independence, and there's a powerful, unconscious wish on Alice's part to keep things as they are.

Soon Tina was on a daily regimen of three solid meals and four breast-feedings. Life was tranquil. Her smiling and cooing behavior was well established and reliable. She had begun to sleep ten hours at night. Alice couldn't believe her good fortune in having such an exciting and satisfactory baby. She felt as if Tina had been around all of her life. How had she ever lived without her?

At five months, feedings began to be more difficult. Tina was distracted by everything, every little sound, every leaf moving on the tree outside the window, every noise from the street. Now she often turned away from the breast to look at her hand or foot. Alice, feeling rejected, called me to see whether or not she ought to wean Tina. I assured her that this was a normal, developmental step, a widening of her cognitive awareness of things around her. It didn't mean that Tina was ready to be weaned. It only meant a growing interest in things around her and that her new awareness competed with her interest in feeding.

    This is the first of many steps toward independence in feeding. It will be a particularly difficult time for Alice, since these signs point to Tina's eventual self-sufficiency. Finger-feeding at eight months, handling and drinking from a bottle or a cup, and using a spoon and fork are all steps that will be hard for Alice to initiate. Alice needs to be pushed a little in order to recognize that Tina is ready for them. Many single parents keep their baby too "infantile" in feeding, nursing them too often and using the breast or bottle as a pacifier. They neglect the stages toward independence and end up with a toddler who refuses to eat, either by being fed or by feeding herself. It is better to reinforce these new abilities as they come along. That way, they are exciting to both the parent and the baby. Otherwise, the same energy, turned inward, makes for a passive or a depressed baby. Turned outward, it may mean subtle, unreachable rebellion later on.

Alice began to find the combination of loneliness and tremendous responsibility all day long more trying. She wanted so much to do right by Tina but constantly felt as if there were things she ought to be doing but wasn't. She looked for perfect ways to do things. When their interaction seemed poor, she felt like an utter failure. When it was good, she wanted to talk about it. She kept in contact with her parents' group and attended meetings weekly. They babysat for each other when an opportunity to get away came along. But away from Tina, Alice felt lost and anxious, so that a date or an excursion away just didn't seem worth it.

&. *Alice needs to work on this part of her relationship with Tina. Being so tied to her baby is not good for either one of them in the long run. If Alice could "learn" about separation in short trials, it won't be as painful later on. Otherwise, Alice might feel compelled to make a clean break, putting her baby in day care too soon and denying her own feelings.*

When Alice did go out, she talked about Tina all the time. She wasn't good company for any of her peers, except those with babies.

&. *Now is a good time for Alice to get back to her sculpture. If she can arrange for a sitter for a couple of hours, or if she can work with Tina around, both of them would profit by it. By developing her own sense of fulfillment, Alice will be more secure, more energized, when she's with Tina. The life of an artist is an isolated one, which may add to Alice's difficulties. By attempting to work out a compromise for a short time, Alice will sense that it is possible to do both and will have the time to look more closely at her options.*

3

The McNamaras

John and Ann McNamara are a hard-working young family. John goes to sea on a dragger sometimes for ten days at a time. When he returns for two or three days, he expects Ann and their three-year-old son Danny to celebrate his return with him. Ann finds this disruption exciting but very hard on Danny. Danny spends most of his time just waiting for Daddy to come home. While John is home, Danny's on a high; then when John leaves, Danny hits bottom. He cries a lot, refuses to eat, and treats Ann like an unwelcome substitute for John. "*My* Daddy told me to do that. *You* are bad," he says, whenever he has misbehaved. "I'll tell my Daddy on you."

Ann works as a typist in a bank. She began working when Danny was a little over a year old. She found what she thought was a good day-care center for Danny and he has been there for two years. She and John need her salary as well as his to make it from one month to the next. Although it was against their religion, they had practiced family planning, because they knew they couldn't afford many children. Nor could they afford having Ann out of work for a long period in order to have a baby.

43

A Second Child

When they knew Ann was pregnant again, they were glad it had happened "in spite of their planning," but they worried about how to make ends meet. Ann felt depressed. How would they manage? It was hard leaving Danny at day care. When she was pregnant with him, she didn't allow herself to think much about it. She and John had been in love for years and knew that when they married they would want a baby. She worried, though, that she might fall into a life of drudgery like her mother, a silent, rather grim housewife who had few pleasures. Her mother had eight children, one right after another, before she realized that she had had enough of her enslaved life. She and Ann's father seemed to accept the constant work as a kind of penance for any small pleasures they had. But Ann saw her mother and father drift apart as she grew up—her father to pubs, her mother into the life of her children. Ann did not want to live that way. She and John wanted a better life for themselves and their children, and they expected to "pay" for it. Only two children, both parents must work—these were decisions they had made then to further their dreams.

When Ann got pregnant with Danny, her image of mothering was of her own mother—always at hand when she was needed, rubbing Ann's back when she was sick, waiting for her at the end of a schoolday. The anxiety of seeing herself as less than this for her own baby was the hardest part of Ann's first pregnancy. She spoke of it only once to John. He was unsympathetic and reminded her of their dream, so she managed to suppress her feelings after that. As a result, she thought of nothing except how they would manage. She faced each day as it came, trying to be interested enough in her job to keep her mind on it. It was easier to work hard at work and at home. That way she had no time to worry, and to "think." When Danny came, he had been a great baby, a great kid, and she had managed. She stayed at home for a year with him and loved every minute of it. When she returned to work, it was hard to leave Danny with other people.

They were on their way to realizing their dream. John's work at sea paid well. Danny was in day care and seemed to like it. Ann was able to manage each day and felt proud. Now, this new baby was going to demand a whole new adjustment. So Ann set her mind to it. But in the back of her mind was the nagging question, How could she ever leave this baby when she had to?

John had felt shut out by Danny at first. Ann had become so absorbed in the baby's care that she seemed to have very little spirit left over for John when he came home from sea. Before Danny came, each return was a real homecoming. Ann waited at the dock for him, completely attentive to him when he finally came ashore. After Danny came, she was always with Danny or at work and, when John came home, acted as if she were angry with him. He felt it was an unspoken anger at the fact that he needed to be away for so long, leaving her to cope alone. He in turn felt guilty that she needed to work—that he alone could not support them. When he returned it seemed like she was competing with him —she talked about her own job, about the news of Danny that she had saved up. He had lost his kingpin role at home. Now, with another baby, he was likely to be even more displaced, blamed even more for their poor financial status. Although she never said it, he was conscious of her comparing her salary with his. He resolved to redouble his working time to help pay for the new baby.

Although they had planned to have two children, the reality of an extra mouth to feed loomed larger. He had been able to figure on supporting and educating Danny without too much hardship. One baby really wasn't a terrible burden. But two babies doubled the expenses, and any fantasies he had had of Ann staying home would have to wait. John tried to get a better job on shore, but his experience was meager. He asked for more work at sea, and that seemed the best they could do. Ann knew she had no choice.

&. *In a way, it's a bit easier not to have to choose whether or not to go back to work. If there's no choice, your mourning can take the form of anger against the system that deprives you of your chance at mothering. Ann will be preparing for the separation all during her pregnancy. No studies have been done that say whether or not this helps the adjustment when it comes, but at least there is little ambivalence to be dealt with.*

The McNamaras are showing their quality. Many young families give up, often resorting to welfare at this point. Our system of supplements seems to reinforce failure, not extra hard work. Had the McNamaras been willing to quit their jobs, separate from each other, and go on welfare, Ann could survive as a lone woman receiving Aid to Mothers of Dependent Children. She could stay at home with about the same margin of cash. If, we as a society could rearrange our priorities, we could offer the McNamaras free day care of a quality that would benefit their children, leaving them free to save a backlog for future bad times. We need to reward families like the McNamaras for their success, not their failure.

Ann knew from the first that this baby would have to be left in someone else's care as soon as she could return to the bank. The bank offered to hold her job for her for a month or six weeks, but they didn't offer any paid leave. She planned to take her two weeks' vacation as part of her maternity leave. If she lost her job, she could draw on unemployment compensation, but this was a pretty meager income to try and live on. John increased his hours aboard the dragger, and they cut down everywhere they could.

When Ann talked to the people at the day-care center, they assured her that they could take the baby along with Danny after four months, but the care would cost over twice as much. They explained to her that staffing a baby room is more expensive because of the ratio of adults necessary for baby care. Most of her salary would go into care for the two children.

Any day-care center that doesn't staff a baby room at a ratio one adult to three or four infants should be avoided. Small babies need more attention than do three-year-olds. The trouble is that day care can cost the equivalent of a mother's entire salary. We need to subsidize day-care centers so that working families can afford quality care for their small children.

The McNamaras didn't see how they could afford such an arrangement, still, Ann was determined her new baby would have as good an experience as possible if she had to leave it so early in infancy. She thought seriously of giving up her job at the bank to stay at home. But she was getting established there and they liked her. Soon she would be up for a raise and a promotion.

Staying away for the baby's sake would postpone that for a year or more.

New Responsibility

John had mixed feelings, both about Ann's job and about this new pregnancy. Both made him feel vaguely put down.

    ❧ The problems of unspoken competition are always present in two-parent families in which both work, whether professional or working class. In one study, boys were unable to identify successfully with their fathers when the mother's job was better than the father's. Mothers unconsciously used it as a lever to gain control over their husbands, and the husbands devalued themselves as a result. The classic sociological study Talley's Corner *demonstrated examples of the self-destructive behavior of black males whose poor self-images led to their failure and resignation. John is feeling the pressure to provide for his growing family. Two children are indeed twice as much responsibility. Since Ann must work, the need and the cost of providing substitute care looms large with a second pregnancy. John is bound to have second thoughts. Ann will have less time for him than ever. Yet, he had so much fun with Danny! Each new stage, every new word, was a joy. Danny's delight at his return each time from sea makes up for a lot.*

John's salary barely managed to cover their basic expenses. Without hers, they had no leeway at all. Postponing the second baby had allowed them some small savings toward a home of their own. When Ann found she was pregnant, their chance to have a home of their own seemed slim. Once they even thought of having an abortion. But neither of them could face that, and they felt extremely selfish to have brought it up. They should be grateful to be having a baby, they felt, and for the most part, they were.

But there were hurdles to cross. At three months, Ann had had some bleeding and was warned to stay in bed or she might lose the baby. Since that meant that she would have to be away from her work, she would use up all her sick leave, so they had to decide whether or not it was worth it to try to save this baby.

Should she "let this baby go" and have another one later? Should she tell her boss about her pregnancy? Did she dare endanger her job? If she took several weeks off now, she'd lose precious time later. They finally decided to take a chance. Ann kept on working, and hoping she wouldn't lose the baby. Her bleeding stopped. They were fortunate, but it made them begin to worry about whether the baby would be normal. Ann began to take better care of herself. She rarely smoked or drank, but they both decided it was too dangerous now. They had read that even inhaling someone else's tobacco smoke might affect the baby, so John confined his smoking to times when he was away from the house.

Ann consulted her mother frequently about what was "safe" for her to eat. She rested at the end of each day. Their life together changed rapidly as they concentrated on this new baby. They never went out at night. Their conversations consisted almost completely of plans for the baby. Childbirth class was a chance to socialize and to share their concerns with other young couples who were in similar circumstances.

There were other concerns. Ann would have to ask for leave when the baby was born. She was afraid her boss might ask her to leave permanently. That would be a blow for them, and they both knew it. What would she do? It took her several weeks before she could muster up enough courage to ask about her future. When she finally did, she discovered that they seemed already to have been resigned to the fact that she was pregnant. They were ready to let her leave for four weeks leave without pay, in addition to her two-weeks' vacation. She was so grateful that she never questioned the length of time. Six weeks seemed like a gift, an eternity, at this time. Despite her experience with Danny, she never considered that she might want more time at home.

When they thought about breast-feeding the baby, she and John quickly gave up the idea. She would have to go back to work so soon; so it was unlikely that she could nurse her baby and work at the same time. Ann felt saddened when she heard the other women in childbirth classes talk about their preparations for breast-feeding. She and John justified their disappointment: John would have "equal time" feeding the baby.

They tried to decide how to divide up their small apartment. Three rooms had seemed enough for the three of them, but not for four. They tried to figure out where they could put the baby's crib. Their bedroom was too small. Danny's room was too small, too, and they didn't want to invade his territory. The living/dining room seemed hardly big enough for anything else. As a compromise, they bought a collapsible crib they could move from one room to another. As gifts of toys and equipment began to pile up, John and Ann found they were surrounded by baby things. There was no place left for them or for Danny. They tried to put a brave face on it, but Ann found she was taking more and more of her own things to her mother's house. The baby's needs were crowding them out. She felt no resentment, just a bit sad for the "old days" of just she and John and Danny. Mostly, she feared the stress on Danny. He was such a good kid. He had to put up with so much already.

Time stretched on. At work, Ann was making a lot more mistakes and often had to retype a page. She hoped no one would notice. She needed to stay on at work as long as she could. John called her at the office a lot to see how she was. She knew he was as excited as she was, but she suspected that the people in her office "resented" her condition, although they were solicitous and seemed interested. Her bosses were too busy to notice. She was so glad to have the job, but she would have been grateful for a word of encouragement from them. She felt so big, so ugly, in everyone's way. When she got depressed, she put her hands on her swollen abdomen. The baby's movement seemed to reassure her that they would all be all right.

John loved being the family comforter. When Ann came home tired and depressed at the end of a working day, he could be amazingly cheerful. He bounced happily around the apartment, cooking for her, comforting her, trying to cheer her up. He treated her as if she were the baby, and she loved it. But he was unrealistic. He said things like, "Don't worry about losing your job. You can easily find another. If you don't, we can make it on my salary." She knew better. How could she get another job in her condition? They needed her paycheck even more now. But she knew John was just trying to make her feel better, so she tried to be more cheerful. It made them feel closer as her time came to an end.

When John was away, she felt very lonely. It was then that she worried about Danny. Danny and his father were so close. Everything was all right when John was home. But suppose she delivered while he was out at sea? What would they do?

The most difficult thing about a second pregnancy is leaving the first child. Was she deserting Danny? She wondered, as she made plans for the delivery. Of course, her fears were irrational, but all mothers grieve for their first child in their second pregnancy.

A Long Labor

When her time of delivery came, John was at home and accompanied Ann to the hospital. He remembered everything he had learned in childbirth class, and kept up a steady stream of instructions—about breathing, about pushing, all in an attempt to encourage her. Her mother-in-law went with them and offered to stay with her when John needed relief. Hospital personnel are prepared for husbands but not for grandmothers. They asked her to wait in the waiting room.

    ❧ Grandmothers are often considered to be an "interference." Most hospitals include husbands in the labor suite but have not yet sensed the importance of the older generation. Medical personnel see grandmothers as a threat to a young mother's independence, rather than a source of support. In most world cultures, the older generation passes on the traditional expectations of the society. They offer boundaries within which the younger generation can find its own way. In our Western culture, the boundaries are so poorly defined that new parents have an unnecessarily difficult time establishing their own values and ways of doing things. It would be easier, during the critical time of childrearing, if we had some guidelines from the older generation. New parents want to find new pathways for themselves, but established limits against which to rebel often help.

Ann's painful labor dragged on. After eight, then twelve, hours, it seemed to John as if she would not be able to hold out much longer. They hadn't been warned of this possibility. Ann was getting tired and discouraged. John was frightened, and tried to get help from the nurses. They said, "It's all right. Many women take much longer." John worried alone, he didn't want to pass his concern along to Ann. She grew more and more weepy. She had always thought of herself as a strong woman, but now she felt like a baby herself.

    ❧ Childbirth education should include possibilities like a long, delayed labor and prepare women for the disappointment of a cesarean section.

After eighteen hours of labor Ann made such poor progress that the young doctor in charge came to a decision. (He had injected pitocin, a drug designed to improve uterine contractions, but to no avail.) Now he would discuss his decision with John and Ann. He and his superiors felt she should have a cesarean section. He called Ann's case "dystocia," an inadequacy of uterine contractions. At this point, they were both ready for anything, relieved to have any decision made for them. But it was a shock—her first labor had been so easy.

    ❧ A long labor is exhausting for the mother but not necessarily harmful to the baby. Labor "alerts" the baby. Even when a surgical delivery is called for, it is probably better for the baby to have been through some labor. Cesarean sections are more common now than they used to be. Brain damage is largely prevented now, and obstetricians are more likely to suggest this course after a long labor. Since it is so common now, it is well to prepare couples for the pros and cons well in advance.

The Older Sibling

The baby, a handsome eight-pound boy whom they named Timothy, was lusty and vigorous. Once at home, he ate greedily, stayed awake a large part of the day, and slept heavily at night. Danny could hardly be comforted. When he saw that his mother was staying home from work with the new baby, he fell apart. He woke up every night crying for his mother and for his daddy. He cried every morning. He had been toilet trained for over a year, but soon began to wet again and to hold back his bowel movements. When Ann tried to help him, he screamed. She thought of letting him stay home with her, but she couldn't stand the turmoil he was causing. She decided that he would be better off at the day-care center where they "cared about him."

&ampnbsp;

Mothers need to be prepared for this. Any older child is apt to regress around the time of a new baby's arrival. In fact, if Danny didn't fall apart, I'd be more worried than if he did. Danny has been making an "expensive" adjustment in day care for two years now. He has done well there and seems to love it, but his behavior shows that his own family comes first. In a way, it's a good sign. It shows how attached he is to his parents, despite all the time away from them.

John tried to stay home to help, but, with extra work on the ship, he could only get home for two days. Ann's mother was too busy to help Ann until three weeks after the baby arrived. Ann looked forward to that as an oasis in the midst of chaos.

The day-care center stepped in when they saw what was happening to Danny. They suggested to Ann that she keep him at home and talk to him about now much she missed him and wanted him with her. They suggested that Ann include him in everything she did for her new baby so he would feel as if he were a part of what was happening at home. It worked. She sat Danny down beside her while she fed Timmy. She asked him to help her diaper the baby. Danny soon began acting like a "big brother." She talked about how she needed him because Daddy was away, and he began to try to live up to her requests. When she asked him to go and get her a clean diaper, he would strut into the next room walking very much like his father. His problems sleeping, feeding, and toileting began to subside as he assumed a real role in the "new" family.

Danny may regress again later on. After all, he's only a baby himself, and this is quite a displacement. But he is showing how sturdy he is by making such an obvious turnabout when given a reasonable chance.

Why didn't Ann foresee this for Danny? Her concern to make it within six short weeks no doubt blinded her to the need to cushion this big adjustment for Danny.

A New Family Takes Shape

As soon as Timothy and Ann were at home and safe, John returned to work, feeling a bit guilty at having been away from the ship for so long. As he left Ann alone with their two boys, he felt the terrible pain of deserting her when she needed him. He hardly dared look back at the three of them as Ann and Danny stood waving to him from the door. He choked down his feelings and set his mind to the goal of providing well for his family. Working helped him keep from worrying. He knew Ann was competent. But he felt cheated himself. Having that deliciously soft little body in his arms was a rare feeling. He called whenever they hit port—to see how Ann and the boys were. When she started to tell him all the new developments—Timmy's smiling, Danny's crying for his dad at night—John cut her short. He didn't realize how jealous and torn he was.

    🙠 Ann could feel slighted by his shortness if she weren't aware of his feelings. She may feel deserted and need to share her decisions. If John can't tolerate her babbling on, she'll feel even more deserted. It is often painful for fathers who must miss out on family events to listen to them afterward. Unconsciously, John longs to participate. On the surface, he's gruff and distant.

Ann's mother arrived for two weeks. She helped Ann adjust to Tim's colicky periods at the end of each day. She got up with him at night so Ann could sleep and became a real second mother to Dan. The whole family latched on to her. She was like an anchor. Ann felt almost ready to take the next step—to go back to work. Even John got home for a long weekend and he and Ann were able to "go out" with each other because Ann's mother was there. All three generations bathed each other in a shower of goodwill.

4
Going Back to Work

The Parents' Choice

Each of the mothers in these first three chapters is asking the same question: "When should I go back to work?" No matter what the situation is, the real issue they face is when to return to work without endangering their baby's development. Although financial and career needs may be pressing, these women cannot ignore their new roles as mothers in making the decision. Both the baby's needs and their own longing to nurture well are critical to their peace of mind as they return to work. Denial is a defense against the pain of giving up a small baby—as it was for the McNamaras—but costs the parents a great deal in their own development.

We find in our own research that there are critical stages of development in mothering. These need to be addressed before a mother returns to work. They may be the same for a father, as well, but so far we have not identified them. Each stage in learning about the other member in the mother–infant pair takes committed time together. Out of this learning grows reciprocal attachment. For the infant, these stages are at the root of what Erikson calls "basic trust" in the environment. For the mother, they may represent basic self-trust as a caregiver.

Once having navigated these stages with her baby, a mother may be more ready to share her baby's further development with another person. A baby may be more ready to learn about important "others." Unless a baby is allowed to experience fully these stages of trust and attachment, his or her ability to attach to important others will be either endangered or diluted—we are not yet sure. We do know, however, just how much these stages need to be respected. In the infant–parent relationships in which these stages are not achieved at all, we see infants fail to thrive— either socially or cognitively and, in extreme cases, physically, failing to gain weight or to grow. René Spitz first described socially deprived infants in institutions in 1945, and since then we have built up a whole literature on the social development of children. We still need to know more about the ingredients in mother–infant attachment, and even more so in the attachment of fathers and infants, but we have come a long way in our means of evaluating relationships and our ability to recognize those that are fulfilling for both infants and their parents.

Very early infancy is the first and most critical time to establish a secure relationship. Within the security of a warm and solid parent–infant relationship, the stresses of everyday living can be more easily handled. The separation that results from work and secondary caregiving can then be balanced with the intimacy that comes at the end of the day. Babies can afford to postpone their "disintegration" until they are reunited with their parent, secure in the trust that their parent will always be there to comfort and reassure them.

How long must a mother (or a father) remain at home in order to develop this kind of security? Each parent will answer this question individually. Understanding their particular relationship with their own baby will help the parent decide. No matter how long, new mothers and fathers need a protected period in which to get to know their baby. Society (see the next section) should make this period possible as a clear option for parents, without prejudice or delayed punishment. New mothers and fathers need different amounts of time to feel securely attached to their baby.

The four stages in the parent–infant relationship, which we have come to recognize as vital to the process of attachment, develop as follows:

1. The first stage usually takes ten to fourteen days. In this stage a mother (or father)* teaches the baby to control his interfering motor and reflex behaviors so that he can prolong his attention to her. She will come to know that, if he is in the proper alert state, she can get him to be alert to her voice and face and to maintain his attention briefly. She learns both the techniques in getting him to the alert state and his own messages to her that tell her that he has had enough (for example, eyes closing or going up in his head, face and body going slack, throwing arms and shoulders back, breathing heavily, yawning, hiccoughing). His facial and body language cues tell her to attain, maintain, and release his attention.

2. The second stage is usually completed in the next eight weeks. During this period, mothers learn how to provide a protective, nurturing "envelope" within which the baby can prolong his attention and learn to respond to her playful interaction. In order to help her baby maintain a long period (several minutes or more) of interaction, a mother needs to do several things: (a) She must choose the right time within the cycle of his other states (sleep, hunger, crying, activity). (b) She must recognize nonverbal cues that say, "I'm ready to play," such as relaxing in his chair or on the bed rather than being squirmy or jumpy; a soft face rather than a searching or tight face; and slowed smooth movements rather than jerky or overshooting ones. (c) She must learn that babies all-too-easily build up to a too-intense reaction to smiles and vocalizations. Her baby is likely to become so involved in his own attempts to respond that he overreacts, startles, and loses the chance to maintain an alert state. By holding on to his buttocks, arm, or leg, she can help him keep himself under control and thereby interfere with his startle reactions. By gently containing him in this way, and by modulating her voice, she can maintain his interest. (d) She

---

*   In this section, I use the feminine pronoun for the parent—although I expect that fathers go through the same stages —and the masculine pronoun for the baby, to avoid confusion.

must learn about his rhythm of high attention—decreased attention—high attention—turning away and recovery—high attention. This rhythm, which, for most babies, seems to take about fifteen seconds to complete, is built on a balance between the high energy (heart and respiratory effort) demanded by intense attention and a short period of recovery, in which demands on his immature system are lessened. Otherwise, for self-protection, an infant will "turn off," rather than be overwhelmed by excitement. A mother who understands this, who drops her voice, reduces her own excitement, turns away her eyes, pulls back in her seat, in a constant, slow, rhythmic way, will help her infant learn how to manage this balance himself. Through trial and error, and intuition, she learns how to engage in a give-and-take that will characterize their future behavior together.

In this rewarding dialogue, the mothers learn to recognize the first faint smiles, the beginning vocalizations, the attempts to lean toward her and to reach for her. All of these responses come into play during this period of two to eight weeks and represent the beginning of communication. As a mother learns to reinforce these responses, she is also learning what *she* needs to know, including the certainty that these responses are indeed produced *for her*. A mother or father who consciously contains a baby, helping him produce a voluntary smile or coo, will already be aware of the effort behind it and will feel appropriately responsible for her or his role in teaching the baby the self-organization necessary to produce these signals.

3.   The third stage starts at about the tenth week and ends in the fourth month. Daniel Stern in New York calls this the period of learning about games, in which the parent learns how to help the baby prolong interaction still further, how to heighten his attention and ability to produce a series of responses—such as a coo or a gurgle, a smile or a laugh, a wriggle or a reaching out. In this period, a baby is learning control, learning how to produce these signals at will in a sequence of three or four at a time. The baby will smile; the mother will smile back. This is repeated with increasing excitement four times, then both will turn away to recover. The infant will coo, the mother will say, "Yes." The baby coos again; she says, "That's right." The baby coos a third time in the silent space she leaves for him. This time his whole body wriggles into the "coo" as it trills upward. The mother responds, "Aren't you wonderful!" They have reached a peak, and both subside to prepare for another "game." By this time, each knows the limits of the game, usually three or four signals alternating back and forth between them. They sense that three or four is the limit. Any more would produce an overreaction in the baby and he would withdraw for good. They are adapting to each other's necessary rhythm, trying out the rhythms of attention they learned earlier, and now they are exchanging important signals when attention is "on." One mother said that she saw her baby as learning about communicating with the outside world in the "on" peak and learning about himself in the "off" recovery period. These rhythmic games are a critical learning experience for the mother or father as well as for the baby.

4. The fourth stage occurs in the fourth month and co-incides with a baby's burst of learning about himself and his world. In this fourth month, an infant becomes acutely aware of novel sights and sounds and is easily distracted from eating, or even sleeping, by whatever is happening around him, during the interaction sequence with his parent as well. He may begin to play by looking at his parent and setting up the usual rhythmic pattern. Then, as if he knows he has her under his control, he turns slightly away to look at his shoe, or at an object over her shoulder. She renews her efforts to capture him, but his eyes glide by her to focus on the other shoe, or over the other shoulder. To the mother, the baby seems tantalizingly just out of reach. What can she do to capture his attention? She tries moving into his line of vision, but he evades her. For minutes at a time, mother and baby play this elusive game, the baby constantly in the lead. If she really wants to capture his interest, she must allow him to take the lead. With a toy, she can play on his newly learned reaching-out technique, coupling it with his new interest in novel sights and sounds, and capture and hold his attention. In this period, she learns that he must be in control and she must resepct his newly emerging autonomy. She can no longer control him; they must share the control over these periods of attention. Having to adjust to her baby's physiological rhythms, she is now prepared for his need to be independent. His bur-geoning awareness of outside events makes him less available

to her. She must learn how to utilize novelty as a way of capturing and holding him.

These four stages of learning about each other lead to a new stage in which the infant is ready for new experiences and for new levels of interaction in which he can take some control. This seems to me to represent a time when a baby is ready for a substitute caregiver. In the first four months, a mother has learned about her baby as well as about herself. When he smiles at her, she knows the smile is *for her*. She has learned to recognize his alert moments, his readiness for interaction, and the rhythms that are necessary to produce responses. I recommend that a mother be at home and available for these four months. Ideally, a father, too, should be freed for as much of this period as possible. As I point out in the next section, a law mandating four months paid maternity leave and one month paternity leave would effectively emphasize the importance of this period.

The first three months are likely to consist of such turbulent adjustments for new parents that their energy is drained. Their baby's predictable periods of colic or evening fussiness cause new parents to feel they have been unsuccessful. They need to get through this three-month period and into the fourth month—the period of playful interaction at the end of the day—and be able to predict when the baby needs sleep, needs to fuss, or can be expected to play. I feel that a mother, or a primary caregiving father, should be free to stay at home throughout these four months in order to "know" the baby. If someone else, in a secondary caregiving role, helps the baby through this period, or if the baby begins to smile, vocalize, and play games for another, new parents will never feel competent or truly "attached" to their baby.

What are the later stages when the stress of separation will likely be at a minimum? If a mother or father can be home longer, is it better? Under ideal circumstances, the longer a parent can be at home nurturing her own baby, the more she will feel he is "hers," and the more intimacy she will feel she shares with him. Each step he makes in his cognitive, motor, or social development with be "hers." The more time she invests in her baby, the more confident she becomes that his responses are *for her*.

If there can be a choice, I suggest a mother choose a time when her baby is not learning a new, demanding task. Once he has consolidated a new step and is in balance again, able to look toward others, he is ready for the disruption of a new caregiving situation. While he is learning a new motor or cognitive task, his resources for social adjustment are being stressed. When the task is mastered, the baby demonstrates a "new" sense of himself, of autonomy. For instance, good times for a change might be (1) at nine to ten months, *after* stranger anxiety and after self-feeding, sitting, and crawling are achieved; or (2) at eighteen months to two years, after walking, negativism, and the heightened fear of separation of the twelve-to-sixteen-month period. Each baby develops at his own pace, so the cues for the appropriate time must come from him. Whenever a mother returns to work, her baby will likely regress to a newly achieved developmental area, but if he has been given early confidence, the regression will be temporary, and the working mother can feel her baby can make it through the inevitable stress of separation.

So far, I have addressed only the subtle psychological cues on which a parent can base a decision about separating. There are many other considerations, of course—economic and practical ones, especially. Women or men who provide an adequate living for their babies are already more secure in their roles. Without this security, the process of attachment may be threatened. Research by L. W. Hoffman with working women shows that a woman who is satisfied with her job and who feels competent in the workplace is a more complete woman and so is able to be a more satisfied wife and more nurturant mother. The same must be true for a man. Being able to face a job with enough energy to do it well and to be gratified by one's performance affects the job of parenting. Thus, the time to return to work must depend in no small way on the opportunities of the marketplace and the work environment.

The psychological well-being of a woman is another consideration. If she is to give of herself to another, wholly dependent individual and to a demanding job as well, she must have her own needs met. Support systems for her become critical. Is she all alone with her baby? Does she have anyone around to back her up in times of stress? Is her husband nurturant to her as well as to the baby? Father participation has an indirect but powerful effect. Grandparents have never been so needed yet so unavailable, for nowadays they often have their own careers and busy lives. Real distance as well as emotional distance may be keeping the new family away from the support of the extended family.

When grandparents are unavailable, it helps if the day-care center can look out for the needs of the parents as well as for those of the babies. If Ann and John could leave Tim and Dan in—and return each day to—a setting that focuses on them as a family, that answers their questions, they would certainly have more security to offer their boys after the day of separation. Alice needs supportive figures in order to gradually break her symbiotic tie with Tina. A caretaker who is willing to share her knowledge about Tina's development and to offer Alice psychological support would make separation infinitely easier for them both.

Thus the circumstances surrounding the separation must be examined. Can the husband of a working wife help keep the family supported and together? If a woman needs to work, she needs a husband who does his share at home or assists in some way.

Over recent years in my practice I have gathered the following practical suggestions from mothers who seem to be doing well at their dual roles:

1.   Adjusting to both roles takes a long time and deserves to. Don't feel under pressure to make it work too soon. With two such important roles, it is worth the energy to sort them out well.

2.   Put a lot of thought into choosing day care or a substitute caretaker. If you can trust someone with your baby, you can invest yourself more successfully in your work. Stay actively involved with the caretaker, at the center or at home. It's important to you and your baby, and to the caretaker as well. But prepare to feel competitive. When you do, remember that your baby can probably manage to adjust to another person, if you can. Don't hesitate to treat your baby your way, and let the other caregiver treat her her way. Your baby will learn to anticipate differences in care, but will be confused by an angry, confused caregiver. You'll have to learn to share, and it's not easy.

3. Save as much of yourself as possible during the day. Sit down when you can. Shut off your mind when you can. If you get tense, try to talk it out or work it out before you get home. Your family needs as much of you as you can muster. The old English custom of tea and a light snack when you get home helps you and your spouse relax. It can be a time when your baby has you both without the tearing demands of mealtime and evening chores.

4. Though it sounds like a cliché, quality of time with children *is* more critical than quantity. A short period during which you are really theirs means more to them than a whole evening of half-distracted availability. Let your children learn early to share in your chores. You can do this by making the chores fun for them to learn with you. Have "children time" and "parent time" clear in everyone's mind.

5. Share housework with your spouse. Housework is not a woman's problem, it is the whole family's problem. If it's important for you to work, it's important for him to help. Sharing half way all along the line may be too rigid, but there are ways to divide up family demands that can be acceptable to everyone. Planning meetings are a must! Sharing feelings are even more important than sharing the work.

6. Plan ahead. Simplify meals and stock the freezer. Don't sabotage yourself by working all night or all weekend. Let the whole family in on the planning and save some special time each day for yourself and your children. If this isn't possible daily, the weekend becomes more critical for "family events." Use each contact to make it as special as possible—meals, the trip home, going to shop, when a child is ill, or on vacation.

7. Have realistic expectations for yourself and your children. It is impossible, or at least counterproductive, for you to try to be a "supermom"—and it costs a child more than it's worth to be pushed too hard to achieve. Making it through, as a caring family working together, may be the most important goal all of you can achieve. If you do, you'll beat the statistics!

A Nation's Choice

When I survey the national climate as it concerns children and their working parents, it becomes obvious that we are far behind many other countries. The governments of Russia, China, and Japan all provide paid maternity leave after the birth of a baby. They also subsidize day care for infants and babies. Many other nations now provide paternity leave or a period that can be apportioned by choice to either parent. Sickness leave can be used by parents when a child is sick or needs them at home for other reasons. These nations are ahead of us in planning for families and children.

Although 55 percent of all children in the United States have working mothers, we Americans seem to resist thinking about it. Perhaps we still wish that women would stay at home and tend to the raising of a family. Other roles for women are not yet sanctioned, or at least seem to deserve no support from the public sector. As one executive said, when I urged him to provide corporate day care for his working families, "It's really the family's problem when the wife has to work. Working mothers ought to pay for it themselves. Then they might find out that they don't come out ahead by working, and stay at home. A woman should raise her own children. If we spent as much as we'd need to provide them with decent day care, we'd be spending too much on one segment of our work force. Older people might feel cheated." None of my arguments—about the need for two incomes in most young families, about including older people in the day care of small children—made any real dent in his thinking. Invariably, he ended up with, "My wife and my mother never worked, and it was better for us as kids. I don't want to give mothers another reason for working."

This unstated and largely unconscious belief that women should stay home dominates U.S. policymaking today. The realities—that families are unstable; that women are at risk without a profession; that most families need two wage earners to survive—are not faced squarely. If they were, we would be looking much more carefully at our responsibility toward young children in substitute care. We Americans cannot afford to have over half of our future citizens, children under five, placed in second-rate caregiving situations. Vulnerable preschoolers are often in unsupervised day care or questionable home care next door. The staff in charge of these impressionable small children are often badly trained. They are so underpaid that the jobs are unattractive to those who can get other work. Though some really do love children, many are there by default. Because budgets are so low, to ask for standards and quality control would put most day care or home care out of business or would price most young parents out of the market. The present threat of sexual abuse in day care is a symptom of the kind of undertrained, unsupervised personnel to whom we are entrusting our small children. The National Association for the Education of Young Children has developed a package for surveillance and for quality control for infant care. They have not been able to implement it, because, by closing centers and devaluing untrained but responsible caregivers, it might do as much harm as good. We need to provide better pay, better education, and higher standards for responsive, educated caregivers for all children of working parents.

As I mentioned before, ideal day care would make the parents' needs just as important as the children's. Opportunities for parent involvement must be there and be considered high priority. Parents should be expected, even required, to participate on some regular basis. They need to be encouraged and welcomed at the end of each day. Peer support group meetings for both parents, in which trained personnel lead educational and heart-to-heart discussions, can provide opportunities to share experiences and to get to know each other. These lateral support groups then become a kind of extended family that supports stressed members of the group during the crises that inevitably will arise.

Meanwhile, business needs to assume a role in the strengthening of the family structure. Providing for the nurturing of new babies is an opportunity to do this. As well, it is an opportunity to strengthen parents' loyalty to the firm. By contributing openly to the maturation of young parents, a firm creates an aura of allegiance and dedication. A company that contributes its share by paying for maternity leave of four to six months, at a minimum, and for a shorter period of paternity leave (four to six weeks), is doing a public service. Parents may not want to exercise these options, but they have the choice, and that is significant. In Sweden, a father can choose to take the maternity leave in lieu of his wife. Provision for leave when a child is ill is a more difficult question, but it needs to be addressed. No parent can be of much use in the workplace when his or her child is languishing at home ill. For most small business and independent work situations, the government needs to subsidize the cost of providing these parental leave options.

Meanwhile, since it is unlikely that business and industry will assume the responsibility, I would like to see us continue to fight for legislation and nationally accepted supports for working families. I would like to see the United States set an example in backing up the efforts of two parents who need to work. We need action at a congressional level to mandate and to subsidize the changes needed to protect the future of our children and our families.

To summarize, I suggest the following national policies:

Paid maternity leave for at least four months. At the end of this period, the mother will know her baby. The baby will be ready for substitute care, which parents can choose thoughtfully.

Paid paternity leave for at least a month. This could be a symbol of the father's importance to his family and as a nurturer of his baby. A father needs to be free to participate in the initial adjustment and to support his wife and learn about his new baby.

Provisions for gradual return to the workplace for mothers who have been at home. Could they be offered shared times or flextimes so that they can make up missed days at a later date?

Disability leave for illness and crises in the family. These could be shared between parents. Each parent could negotiate for times, to fit the demands of the workplace. Days missed could be made up at another time.

Supervised quality child care for infants and small children. It is critical to their future that children be provided with quality care. Ratios of less-than-one adult to three infants or four toddlers are dangerous and likely to lead to poor child development, which we—as a society—cannot afford. We need to demand that day-care or home-care personnel be adequately trained and competent. This means that we must provide for supervisors who can assess day care periodically. It also means that we *must* pay day-care workers an adequate wage and provide them with benefits equivalent to other responsible, trained personnel. Young families with two parents working can rarely afford to pay for quality care and need national or state subsidies. By subsidizing day care, we can demand adequate supervision of our children and their environment, as well as high standards of nurturing care, devoid of sexual and other forms of physical abuse.

Flexible work plans for parents. This means shared job opportunities and flexible times to work, along with being able to spread a work week out to fit the family's needs.

Representative George Miller has created a bipartisan Select Committee of the House of Representatives for Families and Children which is now hearing testimony from all sectors to establish the state of the art in family support. They are collecting disturbing data that show how unwell our society is at present, as measured by its support of family life. They are also collecting ideas for strengthening our national policies for family life. We should all commit ourselves to their efforts, and press for aggresssive legislation to change the present situation.

PART II

Sharing
The Care

5

The Snows

Finding Child Care

Carla had been playing for as much time off as she dared ask for when she decided on one more month. She told Jim what she had done, and, to her surprise, he was delighted. "Good for you, Carla! Maybe she'll get through her colic before you have to go to work." Earlier Jim had criticized Carla's decision to stay home. Now she realized that his criticism really reflected his anxiety about what might happen to Amy when she had to leave.

Carla watched Amy hungrily all day long. That last month she played with Amy as if she were to be banished forever. More and more she hated the thought of leaving Amy, and found it hard to find someone she could trust with Amy. She met many people—older women who were grandmothers, younger women with their own infants, and those at family day-care centers. She even visited the big day-care center near her. But there were very few small infants there, and she wanted a more personalized experience for Amy. And one for herself. She sized up and then rejected each woman, because she felt that she herself could not live with her. She recognized that she needed someone she could relate to as well as someone who would care for Amy.

&. *This is a critical decision. Carla needs a person sensitive to her needs, too. Leaving a small baby is hard. One can expect to grieve for past intimacy and for the stages of development that one will miss. A mother unconsciously feels she is giving up a large part of her baby to someone else, who will get all of the satisfaction of watching her baby develop. She will grieve about the loss and feel a sense of competition. These feelings are inevitable and should be planned for.*

Carla was so critical of all the applicants that for three weeks she found no one. She needed someone only four hours a day, but it seemed to Carla as if she would be giving up all of Amy's waking hours. As the deadline neared, it became obvious that a solution must be found. Jim, in desperation, said one night, "I don't suppose you'd accept me as a caretaker for Amy." Carla replied, "Oh, Jim, would you see whether you could stay here part time?" She seemed so earnest that he gathered his courage and asked his boss if he could have part of each day to work at home. Jim's boss agreed, and Jim felt as if he were presented with an enormous challenge as well as a real gift. To be home alone with Amy part of each day was both frightening and exciting to him. He made Carla go over and over what he should do. Even though he had done everything at least once, it all seemed new to him. On the day Carla actually left, he was in a panic. The first day at home seemed more like forty hours than four hours, but he made it and he felt triumphant. Each day he felt more competent and closer to Amy. Each day he spent hours, it seemed, telling everyone at the office about Amy's latest achievements. Was he becoming a bore? If so, he couldn't help it.

&. *Being alone with and in control of a small baby is very different from just being "on hand." For a man, sharing the baby with the mother present is a lesser responsibility. I found that I always depended on my wife to make the critical decisions when she was there. When she wasn't, I had to face a deeper sense of responsibility in myself. It was so different, when she was away, to be really in charge. My own feelings about being a parent grew stronger, as did my relationship with my child. This kind of experience for Jim and Amy is important for their future relationship.*

An Experienced Caretaker

The next month went by so successfully that Jim and Carla longed to be able to continue to care for Amy in this way. But Carla's boss wanted her back full time, and she knew that eventually they must rely on a third person to care for Amy. This time they both set their minds to it and turned up a warm, loving woman who, having successfully raised two children of her own, seemed "just right" for all three of them. She loved Amy and sensed the difficult adjustment that Amy's parents had to make. She seemed just as ready to help them as she was ready to devote herself to Amy. Each day, when Carla and Jim were about to leave for work, they and Mrs. Warren sat down to plan Amy's day. Together they decided about Amy's solid food, and how many bottles she might have. All agreed that Carla's breast-feeding came first.

᭞ *Breast-feeding can continue if it has been well established and if the mother is determined herself to continue. At least three feedings a day are needed to keep milk coming—one in the morning, one again at the end of the eight-hour day, and one in late evening. The last feeding will probably mean waking the baby. Having nursing to look forward to at the end of a working day makes for a happy and very meaningful reunion. Also, Carla will feel in a special way that she is still important to Amy.*

Mrs. Warren's efforts to include Carla and Jim in planning for the day is a stroke of genius. Even if she doesn't follow their plan precisely, they feel as if they were there symbolically.

When Jim and Carla returned each evening, Mrs. Warren showed them the little diary she kept during the day—to tell them what Amy had done. They felt very much a part of Amy's day.

ॐ Giving up a baby to someone else makes a parent feel more shut out than he or she really is. This is part of grieving. A common defense against this is to detach from the whole situation, not because one doesn't care, but because caring is so painful. Clearly this won't happen with Mrs. Warren, who understands it and won't allow it to happen. By reporting the details of Amy's day, she keeps Carla and Jim involved. It isn't likely that they will engage in the inevitable competition and criticism of her that might develop otherwise.

Mrs. Warren kept Amy up longer in the morning. That way, Amy took long late afternoon naps. By the time Carla and Jim got home at 5:30, Amy was wide awake and ready for their evening together. This was a wise and thoughtful move on Mrs. Warren's part, and Carla felt taken care of as well. They had indeed landed in a tub of butter with Mrs. Warren!

ॐ The readjustment had been easier than any of them expected. Coming home to someone so mature, motherly, and caring was pure joy. Many older women are unconsciously angry at young mothers who "desert" their young. This anger and competition interferes with their ability to nurture young parents who need it as much as the baby does. The ideal sitter is one who, like Mrs. Warren, knows that her job is to cement the whole family together, not just care for the baby.

Carla was much more certain of herself at work now. She was more assertive and able to make good decisions more quickly. She had to keep herself from feeling sorry for the young, unwed males in her office who had no "Amy" at home. She realized she was more competitive than she had thought.

❧ *Gilligan, in her excellent book,* In Another Voice, *presents the psychodynamic insight that women learn to compete in ways different from those of men. Men compete directly and openly. Women do it by turn-taking and other more indirect techniques. Matina Horner points out that women are "afraid" of success because it uncovers the uneasy recognition that, with success, one threatens others. Women's roles are supposed to be nurturant and noncompetitive. Carla must recognize her own competitiveness in order to accept her success. Now that she is facing the "decision" to be successful in two areas, she must deal with being a "superwoman," superior to men in two ways. This is scary for Carla. Will she have to hide it from Jim? Can she?*

At the same time, Carla's mind was not on her work. She constantly dreams of being at home. At the end of the day she was exhausted by her efforts to be mentally in two places at once—at home and in the office. She worried that the quality of her work had deteriorated. This deep-seated dichotomy—feeling both more assertive and at the same time less competent—was unnerving and frightening. It was some reassurance, however, when her boss congratulated her on how well she had adjusted. She desperately hoped he meant it, for she herself wasn't all that sure. How often she felt like running away to a lonely deserted island where no decisions had to be made! She often felt like weeping, especially when she had to go to the ladies' room to milk herself in order to keep her milk coming. Calling home to "touch base" with Mrs. Warren was, she realized, for her own sake. She felt only half alive all day without Amy. At night, she pushed in to pick Amy up and hold her, under so much steam that it frightened Amy. In Carla's arms, Amy cried and seemed to say, "You scare me!" Carla was frightened and felt shut out by Amy's response. "Was Amy angry at having being left? Had she herself been shut out of Amy's life?" Mrs. Warren gently pointed out to Carla that her eagerness simply overwhelmed Amy. Carla realized that by slowing down she could prevent Amy's overreaction.

Jim also felt shut out, but in a different way, when he returned to work. It had been gratifying to stay home with his baby. She had been "his" in the way he had dreamt about during Carla's pregnancy. Now, on weekends, it was hard once again to get up courage to bathe or feed her, tasks that had seemed so easy when he was alone at home with her before. It seemed as if each event was too heavy with symbolic meaning for him. When he managed to conquer these feelings, he saw that Amy loved the situation and was thriving.

One day, though, she started crying for no reason. He felt a panic he could barely contain. What could *he* do to satisfy her? After all, he was only a man. He realized he had always seen himself as a second-rate mother or babysitter; he could deal with Amy only when things were going along well. When she needed real nurturance, when decisions had to be made, he just couldn't see himself as being capable. Should he call Carla? or Mrs. Warren? When he remembered that he had cared for Amy alone, he paused and looked at her more carefully. She helped him find the answer he needed. She was desperately tired, over-loaded, and needed to sleep. In bed, she cried briefly, then snuggled into the bedclothes. Putting her thumb in her mouth, she went off to sleep. Jim felt like a conqueror. After that day, he gathered up more and more courage to find his own solutions. He assumed responsibility with Amy, and she and he both re-alized it. They settled into a different, more comfortable rela-tionship.

&. *This unconscious "measuring-up," comparing them-selves against the "all-knowing female," is a way men have to keep themselves subordinate in the nurturing role. In the pro-cess, they are likely to abdicate the real responsibility they need to feel to achieve a comfortable and sure relationship with a child. Recognizing himself as a competent caregiver, being able to decide for himself what Amy needs, is a big step for Jim.*

Women adjust more easily than men. They have been reared to think of interdependency as critical to all of their relationships, and sensitivity to others is expected of them. This is not part of a man's early experience, but like a gift, comes with being a father.

Crisis

Amy seemed able to adjust to everything. The transitions made in the first six months had been successful, and parenting now seemed like a breeze. Carla's job was going so well. She felt so complete when she came home and scooped Amy up in her arms that she wondered why she had waited so long to return to work. Jim was on top of the world. Every evening he rushed home to tend to Amy. He left the supper to Carla while he played and chortled with the baby in the living room. Weekends, without Mrs. Warren, were so much fun it seemed like playing house. The weekends were a dividend—two adults, free of work, playing with their baby, sharing the housework and cooking, yet aware that Monday was just around the corner. On Mondays they escaped the household chores; relieved of having to feel so utterly responsible for Amy; glad to be returning to their exciting jobs. They were like children who could have everything their own way. Why did people make such an issue out of having a baby? They loved every minute of it, and began to plan for their next baby.

One morning Mrs. Warren called to say that her own daughter was seriously ill and that she must go to her. She had several grandchildren who would need her, so she'd be there for some time. She hated to leave the Snows and had called her friends looking for someone to replace her, but wasn't able to turn up anyone. Could they manage? She would let them know as soon as she could about coming back, but, at present, she doubted she could. The Snows assured her they could manage and she should not worry. But if she could return, they would greet her with open arms.

The axe had fallen. Carla called off her appointments. Her colleagues groaned. She knew it was up to her to stay home. She told Jim that she felt it was her responsibility. He protested, but not very vigorously.

&. *The division of labor is never completely equal in most families. Mothers are expected to feel more responsibility—and they do. In the workplace, women are more easily forgiven for taking time off for their baby. Men are more likely to be consciously or unconsciously criticized.*

By the end of her first day with Amy, Carla was ready to scream. She had forgotten how much work there was to be done. The house needed cleaning. There was food to prepare. Amy seemed constantly upset. Carla found herself resenting Jim's absence. She was overwhelmed by Amy's demands and by her own feeling of being the only one responsible for her. At night, Jim faced a grim, angry woman and a whining child. Neither one had had a good day. Jim spent hours on the phone trying to rearrange his life so he could stay home half a day to relieve Carla. He was only partially successful. In two days, he promised he could stay home every afternoon. Meanwhile, Carla would have to be in charge—unless they could get a sitter. They called around, but were always disappointed. The only person they could turn up promised to be available in a week but wanted a very high salary and preferred older children. After the third day, Carla was almost desperate enough to hire her, but her better judgment prevailed.

     ❦ In a crisis, the care of the baby almost always falls on the mother. To be angry with Jim helps Carla ventilate her frustration; but the truth is, she feels it's her responsibility and it's up to her to meet it. Part of her anger at Jim is really at herself. She knows she's not yet playing both roles well—her job and mothering. She has more to learn about mothering, and this crisis is a reminder that she's got a lot farther to go. If only she could have stayed home longer in the beginning, she might have felt more secure now.

Being away from her job weighed heavily on Carla's mind. She felt she was missing so much of her work that she would never catch up. The world was slipping out from under her; she was no longer adequate to handle anything. Her desperation made her feel more helpless. Finally, Carla pulled herself together and realized this wasn't the end of the world—"just" another crisis. She would catch up.

Amy was getting pretty upset by all this tension. At seven months, she was already sitting and playing alone for long periods of time. But now she had begun to fall helplessly over on her side whenever Carla tried to leave the room. She wanted to be held or carried most of the day. As Carla got more tense, Amy got more demanding. At times, Carla felt like screaming right along with the baby. Mealtimes were no fun either. Amy grabbed at everything—the spoon, the cup, the dish of cereal, smearing it in her hair. She was like someone Carla had never seen before.

When she put Amy to her breast, she felt tense and angry. Amy knew it and fought at Carla's breast so that feedings were no longer a shared time. Neither one spoke to the other. Amy seemed determined to make life hell for Carla.

Nights Amy began to wake up screaming. Jim rushed to her, sure she was in pain. He picked her up and held her sobbing against his shoulder. She managed to gasp in his arms for thirty long minutes. To Carla, each gasp felt like a knife in her side. Jim tried to comfort Amy. "Darling, what's wrong? What has happened to you? Have you and Mommy had such a bad day?" After thirty minutes, he angrily blamed Carla for frightening Amy by her own anguish. Carla fell onto the couch in the living room, putting the pillow over her head to shut out their voices. She felt like leaving them both.

The days dragged on. No word from Mrs. Warren. No luck with a replacement. Jim finally carried out his promise. He would set it up so Carla could work half a day, while he stayed home.

This worked out for a while, but it was a complex arrangement for all of them. To catch up, Carla and Jim each added two more hours onto their half day at work, so there was little time for being together. Jim went to his office at 6 so that he could be home by noon. Carla and Amy got up after Jim left in the morning. Carla came home two hours late, in order to finish up her work at the office. She arrived after Jim and Amy had finished their dinner and after Amy had gone to bed. Neither Carla nor Jim were pleased with the situation, nor could they help each other to adjust to it. Amy continued to wake up at night. It was hard to feed her or put her to bed. She seemed to be as upset as they were. No one seemed able to pull the family together.

Grandmother's Help

After the second week, Carla, in desperation, called her mother. Mrs. Hunt dropped everything and came over. She fed Amy effectively, allowing her to play with her food, and helped her to try to feed herself. She calmed her down at night. She showed Amy how to play by herself again. She put herself at Amy's disposal and nurtured Carla and Jim as well. She soothed their tensions, listened to their sorrows, and sent them back to work. When they came home, everything was in order.

&. *Once the emergency is over, however, Carla may feel guilty that she hadn't been able to cope. Jim may feel guilty that he failed to settle things himself. They both need to use this peaceful time to reorganize. They had both become too dependent on Mrs. Warren and had essentially assigned her the role of mothering all three of them. Now it's time for them to develop more responsbility for Amy and for each other. This shake-up can be good for them as a family—they can learn from it—or it can be a source of friction between them. Each needs to assume a more active role in the household and, for Amy's sake, begin to see her as theirs, not Mrs. Warren's. Reassigning roles is a dangerous part of returning to work. A working mother may give up her self-image as mother of her baby, feel shut out and lost. She may feel unnatural and inadequate in the role of mothering when she has to return to it in a crisis such as this.*

Carla's mother suggested that she and Jim come home on time at night, so they could begin to "know Amy" again. "After all," she said, "she is your baby, and she's been through a lot of changes. You need some relaxed time together." They might have gotten angry at her frankness, but they knew she was right, so they listened and began to watch her with Amy. Carla realized that it had been a long time since she had watched for Amy's new developments. She had been treating her like the three-month-old infant she had left in Mrs. Warren's care. At seven months, Amy was an entirely new person and intended to be treated that way. She wanted to help feed herself. She wanted to hold a cookie and a spoon while solids were being fed to her. She tried to help with the breast-feeding and wanted Carla to communicate with her during feedings. At night Amy woke once. Mrs. Hunt said to Jim, "Come and speak to her, but you don't need to pick her up. She just needs to know you are here." Jim began to feel needed once again. Each day he rushed home to see what Amy had learned. They all began to settle down and to feel that they were together, unified as a family once again. But what would happen when Carla's mother had to leave?

&. *Another problem with a working parent's tidy solutions is that, during a crisis, they may not work. The balance that had been so carefully achieved for the day-to-day routine hasn't enough flexibility in it to allow for the crises that are bound to occur. When a child is sick—when any part of the system breaks down—a parent needs to be available. And that's not always possible. It makes minor crises seem like major ones. Couples like Carla and Jim feel like they're skating on thin ice. It's just not easy to raise a family and hold down two jobs at the same time.*

Day Care

Carla realized they had better find a more permanent solution. Mrs. Warren had been so dependable, but emergencies do occur. Having a grandmother around was a luxury. Now it was time to arrange for day care. Carla called friends who had small children for suggestions. There were no openings anywhere. The good day-care centers had long waiting lists. Carla was up against the wall.

&. *Providing substitute care for a baby is difficult, whatever one's circumstances may be. The number of day-care centers is grossly inadequate (about 10 percent of small children can be provided for at present), and their quality unpredictable. Most children of working-class couples are delegated to neighbors or others who offer care in their homes. These people are inadequately trained and supervised. In many subsidized centers, the staff is poorly paid, overworked, and not very interested in children. Even for middle class couples who can pay full fare, opportunities for care are sparse. Carla will have to check out several centers before she makes a decision. She's at the mercy of too few places and may not find an ideal one.*

Jim called the Associated Day Care Association for a list of qualified centers. He and his mother-in-law took Amy with them to look at three of the most likely ones. One was already overcrowded; the ratio of babies to adults was five-to-one. That was unacceptable to Mrs. Hunt.

The second day-care center they visited was delightful. There were six babies in the baby room. Amy looked at each of them with glee. The two workers there seemed competent and sensitive to each baby. Crying babies were picked up and carried or held. They sat in chairs that faced each other and were encouraged to interact with each other. The atmosphere was warm. Jim and his mother-in-law felt good about this one. The staff, having seen Amy, couldn't resist her and were intrigued by a father who was so involved. They offered to take Amy. Then Mrs. Hunt asked if she could inquire about something. Everyone stopped to listen. She said, "I know I'm acting like a grandmother, and I apologize in advance. But I'm concerned about my daughter's development as a mother. She's a competent lawyer, but hasn't had much experience yet as a mother. I worry that she'll leave Amy to you and, in her mind, won't take responsibility. Is there anything you can do here at the center to keep Carla involved?"

Jim was aghast, yet he knew what she meant. He remembered how he and Carla had depended on Mrs. Warren and how they had fallen apart when she left. The day-care director said they encouraged new parents to take an active role in the baby's room once a week. Jim volunteered, and promised his wife would do the same.

&⬩ *It is critical that parents continue to be in charge. It is too easy for them to assign the responsibility for their baby's development to "someone else." Carla and Jim, like any new, inexperienced parents, needed a push. The fact that this center is prepared and eager to have parents participate is an excellent sign. Here, the needs of the whole family will be met.*

Carla's mother left them with the feeling that they were back on the right track. She had served them well, and they knew it.

&⬩ *Caring grandmothers are all too rare. At a critical time Mrs. Hunt pressed for the help she knew they needed. Now they can start afresh, developing together as a family.*

The day-care center worked out well. Carla spent one day a week with Amy in the baby room. She and Jim both found it to be a rewarding experience, and good for Amy. The difficulties they had had with Amy around feeding and play began to clear up as they watched these competent people with seven different babies. Carla and Jim learned how to handle the other babies as well as their own. In fact, as they became more involved with children and child development, they began to feel like "experts" at it. They read books and watched television shows about babies and discussed child development at every meal. They both felt the zeal of a new interest.

Amy thrived in this new climate. She chortled all evening and slept all night. But she hated to be left at day-care each morning. Carla and Jim took turns taking her in and knew she would fuss and cry when they left. They felt like child-deserters but were assured that Amy settled down as soon as they were out of sight. After a few weeks she started to look forward to the center. Then they felt a little jealous. She had stopped crying when they left her, and began to fuss when they picked her up at the end of the day. Carla thought Amy hated to leave the center. Jim thought she was showing her anger at them for leaving her. (I discuss this more fully in the next chapter.)

One evening, as they were dressing Amy to leave the center, she screamed as if she were hurt. Carla nearly dropped her. A member of the staff came over to see what was wrong. As soon as Amy saw her, she stopped fussing, grinned, and put out her arms to her, as if to say, "Take me away from this monster, my mother." Carla felt terrible, and the woman immediately realized what was happening. She said, "You know, I think Amy is just mad at you. She's teasing you by appealing to me. Let's try it. I'll take her as if she had to stay here. I bet she'll change her tune in a hurry!" As the woman carried her off, Amy looked back at her mother in horror and with a terrible wail. She reached out toward Carla, as if to say, "It's really you I want." Carla took Amy home whistling.

&. *Working mothers need constant confirmation that their babies really need them. A working mother feels so torn and grieved at losing part of her baby's day that she feels less than adequate. When the baby's behavior seems to reprimand her as well, she feels it so deeply that she is likely to overreact and withdraw even more. It is critical that secondary caregivers be aware of this and explain the baby's behavior to the mother. Cementing the family together ought to be the primary mission of a day-care center. Otherwise, it may split a family apart without meaning to.*

Carla and Jim are conscious now of the kind of energy and time they need to save for Amy at the end of the day. Each of them has learned a lesson. They plan their working days with the end of the day in mind. Jim wants to have the energy to play with Amy, to bounce her up and down and make her giggle happily, despite Carla's admonition that "she'll never get to sleep."

6

The Thompsons

The "Extended Family" of Day Care

At Tina's next visit a month later, Alice said, "Well, now you've really got to help me. I must get back to my studio. I've been putting it off all this time, because I couldn't face it. But I think I can stand to share Tina now. I need to work—to keep my sanity as well as my self-respect. I had plans for a show before Tina was born, but haven't done a thing since. I need to get back to teaching as well, to make ends meet. Wouldn't it be better for me and for Tina if I learn to leave her with others now? I knew you'd tell me straight. You were so hard on me before."

I thought Alice probably wanted me to tell her to stay with Tina longer, but I knew she needed a push in the direction of independence, and I could see that this was fast becoming my major role in helping this pair. So we explored the issues—what kind of care for Tina would she need? Where could she get it? How could she be sure it was quality day care, not just a place to dump Tina every day—she couldn't stand that. I pointed out

85

to her that she might look for a place where she herself felt protected and cared for. She looked at me in complete surprise. "You mean I might spend time there, too?" It turned out that Alice simply thought day care was a place to drop Tina off and leave as quickly as possible. I pointed out that, because it was so painful for her to leave Tina at all, she probably just felt like running away from the issue of separation. It wasn't necessary, and wouldn't be good for Tina. A gradual adjustment, would serve the dual purpose of freeing her for work and helping Tina learn to adjust to other adults and children. I pointed out that, in Tina's case, there was more reason for an "extended family" in day care than for a child in a larger family. "But," I added, "there's reason for you to feel a part of this extended family of day-care, too. Look what it's meant to you to know the other single parents." She nodded appreciatively.

We discussed the possibilities for substitute care, and settled on a family day-care center nearby that one of her new friends— another single parent—had used and felt very positive about.

≈ Family day care can be one of the most supportive kinds of day care. A woman at home usually takes two or three infants into her own home to care for them along with her own. The personalized care that is possible, as well as the close contact between caregiver and parent, can be real assets. Of children presently in day care 75 percent are reputed to be in such family day care. For a good description of this type of care, see E. Galinsky and W. A. Hooks, The New Extended Family: Day Care That Works. *It can also be dismal, if the day-care person is overwhelmed by too many children, or if she is not really interested in the development of the child. It can be just a parking lot with the children in front of a television set. It can, on the other hand, be like an extended family. Mothers can participate freely and helpfully; they can come and go at will. Family day care is less expensive, but there is likely to be less supervision over the quality of care. The National Association for Education of Young Children, in Washington, D.C., is attempting now to set up minimal training standards for operators of such centers, and for teams of supervisors to maintain these standards. In these at-home centers, it is even more important that parents stay involved to ensure optimal care for their child.*

Staying Involved

I urged Alice to look into it, and I reminded her that Tina's well-being is still her responsibility and that if she did decide on a small center, she would have to stay involved. She'd need to use her judgment all along to decide that this was "right" for Tina.

&. *One serious problem in day care is that a parent begins to withdraw from participation in the center. They simply turn the child over to the center. This happens, not because they don't care but because they care too much. Caring too much hurts. Any parent who must share her small child with another care-giver will grieve. She will feel guilty, inadequate, helpless, hope-less, and even angry at having to give up her child. "Why me?" No matter how well she has rationalized the separation and how necessary it may be, these feelings will arise. There are three inevitable defenses against these feelings of powerlessness and guilt: (1) denial—denying that it matters, either to you or to the child; (2) projection—projecting all the good mothering onto the day-care person and taking all of the bad for yourself, or vice versa—becoming unnecessarily jealous and competitive with the other caregiver; and (3) detachment—pulling out to leave the baby in the other's care—not because you don't care, but be-cause it hurts so much to care. These defenses are necessary and inescapable, even with excellent day care. The more satis-factory the substitute care is, the more competitive you will feel, and the more these defenses will be necessary. It isn't possible to get rid of them, but it is necessary to know they are there and likely to dominate your behavior. Otherwise, you are liable to interfere with perfectly adequate care for your child. Staying in touch and participating in your child's day-care is the hardest job of all—because you care so deeply.*

Alice and I discussed these issues. I knew she would need to hear them from me over and over again. If she could begin to realize the depth of her feelings and to share them with me, she needn't be at the mercy of them. For I knew already how deeply she cared about Tina and about doing a good job of mothering her. Alice was becoming more and more a person in front of my eyes.

Overcoming a Label

She said, "How can I tell what kind of place would be good for Tina? Should I tell them I'm a single parent, or would that prejudice them against me—and her?" I asked her why she felt she should hide it, and we talked again about how comfortable she felt with her role. I reminded her that, although she had been almost aggressive about it when she first came to me, now she seemed pretty easy with her own side of it.

"For me, I think I am. But for Tina, I'm not so sure yet. I suddenly want to protect her from having to pay a price for my problems. I don't want her to be teased for having no daddy, and for having a mother who flaunts society."

We discussed this at some length. Of course, Tina would be in for this kind of labeling by adults and later for teasing from children her own age. There was no way that Alice could protect her from t. But what she could do was be open and straight with Tina, so that Tina would know she could come to her mother when she felt besieged. Also, and most important, if Alice feels easy with herself and their place in society, she won't wince or pass on to Tina the sense that Tina is a less-than-adequate member of society. By the time Tina is four or five, when all children tease each other, Alice should be ready to say. "You live with your mommy and not your daddy. There are plenty of kids like you, and you and I are doing just great together. All kids tease and like to be teased. Tease back. You don't need to believe that you aren't okay."

&. *I find that all small children go through the same self-questioning. We can all remember our doubts as children. "Am I really adopted? Am I really a boy or a girl? Am I okay or not?" No matter what the label may be, someone will always be there to question one's integrity. Children of this age need to explore all the possibilities. If a parent wants to help—and Alice will need to—she must be ready with her own, sure sense of competence and sense of the rightness of their lives. It is never too soon to get ready for this—it's always a shock to a parent.*

This self-questioning does not spare any child—if he's blond, why not brunette; if he's black, or Latin, why not Caucasian; if he's Caucasian, why not something else; if she's a girl, can't she

*ever be a boy? If there is a real issue—such as Tina will have—
it is all the more critical that the parent be prepared. A child
with a birthmark, for example, will need extra back-up at age
four to six when children are searching so hard for their iden-
tities.*

Evaluating Day Care

I hadn't answered Alice's questions about day care, because I
wanted to seize the opportunity to discuss her feelings about
being a single parent. So we returned to that issue. I suggested
that she visit some of the places she was considering. Alice
should check on issues of health and safety. Is it clean? Are
there adequate safeguards over the electric outlets?

     *❧ She can observe these things without asking any ques-
tions. If she wants to pursue it further, she has a perfect right to
ask, "What would you do in an emergency? How could you leave
three children in order to tend to one injured child?" She could
and should test the woman's preparations and her ability to act
appropriately in an emergency. In addition, Alice should ask
herself, How would I like to spend a day here? Do the children
here look hungry or too restless? Do they look as if they are
having an interesting and cared-for experience? Or are they
empty-looking, bored, and crying out for someone to pay attention to them? Working mothers need to look for a caregiver's
sensitivity to each baby's cues. Is she sensitive to each one as
a person, or does she have a fixed idea of what "any child"
needs? Does your child like her, or is he or she more guarded
than usual? Ask the caregiver whether she recommends a gradual or an abrupt separation. If she doesn't want you and your
toddler or baby to take your own time in separating, you don't
want to be there. It's a difficult transition for both mother and
child, and mothers need to be sensitive to it. Otherwise they feel
guilty, and inevitably withdraw. Be sure a caregiver cares about
you as well as your baby—or your naturally competitive and
angry feelings will endanger your relationship with her—and
your baby may suffer as a result.*

When visiting a day-care center or home, watch a mealtime or a busy play activity. Can the caregiver manage all the different personalities and respect them at the same time? Or is she overwhelmed? Does she become rigid and impersonal when there is much to be done? Any day with small children is fraught with crises—and with three or four small ones, a caretaker needs patience, flexibility, and humor. Are the different cycles of different children managed adequately, or are they all lumped together? When there are different ages in the same center, this becomes even more of a problem. Lastly, is there extra help for all these children, or does the caregiver try to manage them all alone? Can she call in another set of hands or another warm heart? If not, be careful about ratios of more than three babies to one adult. Individual treatment will be the first thing to go.

Can you afford quality care? My thought is that you can't not afford it. Alice will be financially stressed, but if she leaves her baby in a less-than-optimal situation, she won't be able to tolerate it and her work will suffer. If Tina has problems later, Alice will blame herself for leaving her. Since all children are bound to have some problems, Alice had better be sure she has done her best by Tina.

I noticed that, as we talked about these searching issues, Tina had been lying in Alice's lap looking up at her mother's concerned face. Her small face was lined with a frown. As Alice talked, she patted Tina with more and more vigor, as if she needed to be sure she was still there. Finally, Alice looked down at Tina. "Mummy will see that you're okay. It won't be easy, but we can do it." She smiled, and Tina grinned back at her. There was a sense of relief. Tina's little hands grasped her mother's fingers and held on tight.

The First Separation

By the time of Tina's sixth-month visit, the issues were being settled. Alice had a teaching job lined up. But it did not start for a while and her own work was flexible. She realized, as she began to get Tina adjusted, that this was truly a blessing. To be able to separate slowly made it easier—taking her a few hours the first few days, returning to feed her lunch. The first day, she felt at first as if she were entering a prison. She'd had dreams of deserting Tina, of leaving her on a deserted but dangerous road. The day of their separation, she walked around with a lump in her throat, unable to eat or drink. She clutched Tina to her so tightly that the baby began to cry. When she realized how upset Tina was, she called two of her single friends to consult with them. They reassured her that she could do it; that it had been just as painful for them.

When she got to the house, she felt like bolting and going home. Mrs. Marlin, the woman who cared for the babies, was so warmly receptive that she soon dispelled Alice's fears. "Why don't you stay for this morning and just do all of the things I'll be doing with Tina when you're not here. Then you can think of where she is and what she's doing whenever you miss her. I'd like her to get used to my place with you anyway."

    This kind of sensitivity to Alice's feelings and to Tina as a person "even though she's only six months" is a wonderful bulwark against Alice's anguish. By welcoming her and urging her to be there, Mrs. Marlin is acknowledging the bond between mother and baby. It also lets Alice feel that Mrs. Martin is not hiding anything from her as a parent. I urged Alice to get Tina there early each morning for a while, so they can get adjusted together.

Stranger Awareness

She was able to stay nearby when Mrs. Marlin took over after Tina's nap. Although it was obvious that Tina recognized Mrs. Marlin as a stranger, she learned to accept her while her mother was nearby. It all seemed to go smoothly, and Alice went off to her studio at noon, feeling like a new person.

    It is foolish to think that small babies don't "know" strangers and strange handling. We think they show patterns of recognition for strangers by the fourth to sixth week. There are peaks of heightened stranger-awareness and anxiety that need to be respected in planning a transition such as leaving a child in day-care or with a new stranger. At four and a half months or thereabouts, children are highly aware of objects and people. Some become wary of new places and new people at this time. I see this in my office when a mother puts her undressed infant on my examining table. If I'm not careful to keep the mother's face in full view, the baby will dissolve in tears at my strange one.

At eight months, most children demonstrate real anxiety if a stranger descends on them or tries to do anything for them that is too intimate. This period is associated with the increased independence that comes with the ability to locomote. Object permanence, as described by Piaget, is also associated with this. That is, babies can conceive of their mothers or fathers being nearby even if they are out of sight. As researcher Harriet Rheingold says, don't invade an eight-month-older's private space. Wait for him or her to come to you. Then you'll avoid the wrath of eight-month stranger anxiety.

At one year, with the advent of cruising and walking and its concomitant independence, accompanied by an increasing sense of autonomy, toddlers are likely to be very worried about new situations. These three ages should be avoided as much as possible, if there are choices, in instituting a new caregiving situation.

Children are always sensitive to separation and one should respect their need for cushioned transitions, but other times aren't as likely to be traumatic.

New Adjustments

The teaching and sculpting and the new caregiving situation seemed to blend very well. Alice felt almost liberated. She felt light-hearted, carefree, and guilty that she enjoyed it so much. Her colleagues were glad to see her back. They seemed proud of her and asked her in detail about Tina and how she was doing. Although the more conventional ones seemed to be looking for flaws, they could sense how successful Alice felt about her baby. She glowed as she talked about Tina, and no one could resist the joy she felt in her baby. One young man seemed to want to be in on their joyful relationship and quizzed her daily about Tina's progress. She found she had come to a whole new level of personal adjustment and could afford to be maternal and magnanimous to people she used to run away from.

Weekdays went very well, and weekends were a time of reunion. Tina was joyful to have her mother all day to herself. By Sunday, however, Tina became very excitable. She wanted to be up all day and was fussy in the evening. By nighttime, Tina was exhausted, and Alice was frantic. Why had Tina fallen apart? Why hadn't she known what to do to get Tina organized? She felt relieved that Monday—and Mrs. Marlin—were right around the corner. But she slept badly, waiting for Tina to rouse and to need her.

This may be a delayed reaction to the substitute care. Children have an amazing ability to adjust, but at some expense. They may not show it at the time, but fall apart later. The difficult thing is that it compounds Alice's feelings of inadequacy and she wants to get away. Mothers like Alice need constant reassurance. They constantly need to explore their feelings about leaving a baby to someone else.

Tina settled down again in Mrs. Marlin's care. She fell back into the routine each week as if it were a relief to get back. Alice sensed this and took it personally. Tina began to fuss at the end of each day just as Alice arrived at Mrs. Marlin's house to get her. Frantic, she called me for advice. "Tina likes Mrs. Marlin better than me. She is either angry at my leaving her, so she fusses when I return, or else she really doesn't want to leave Mrs. Marlin. Mrs. Marlin says she never fusses that way for her during the day. I'm scared I've lost her already."

Researchers in our Child Develpment Unit at Children's Hospital observed babies in day care over an eight-hour stretch. They seemed to function at a rather low key all day long—not getting very excited or very fussy, and not sleeping very deeply. It was as if they were guarding themselves against getting too involved in any part of their day—until their parents came to get them at night. Then they let go! They cried loudly, almost angrily, saving up their strong emotions for the people who mattered to them. Their tired, "disintegrated" parents ran headlong into this barrage. They felt guilty, blaming themselves, and took their baby's crying as a personal response to their having been left. At this point, someone in day care always turned to the guilty parent to say, "She hasn't cried like that all day!" In other words, "It must be you who makes her cry. We don't." Parents are all too vulnerable, and this tends to distance them from their babies. If, on the other hand, they are made to understand that their baby has saved up important messages and feelings all day, they go home feeling important to the baby. And they are ready to enjoy the sequel to the crying period—a long period of alert, responsive interaction, saved up all day, too.

I was able to help Alice sort out these feelings on the phone. Her relief was obvious, for she had been coupling her new satisfying life with increasing guilt over having left Tina. We talked about how these issues would surface from time to time and how she might need to call me periodically to help her sort them out.

Priorities

The question of "quality time" with Tina came up, and we discussed it at the next visit. Alice was aware of the fact that, as she got involved again with her work, she had less energy left over at the end of the day for Tina. I warned her that this wasn't fair to Tina. She *must* save some of herself for the end of the day. And she *must* arise early enough for a leisurely interaction with her baby. Recently she had been letting Tina sleep late in the morning, rushing her over to Mrs. Marlin to be fed and skimming off to her classes just in time.

I reminded here that only one month before she had been mourning about leaving her baby at all. Now she seemed to be withdrawing from Tina into her work. Was that what she really meant to do? She complained about how hard she worked, about how much she needed a social life. I admitted that I was sure she was pressed, and that she needed and would be wise to learn how to pace herself. But her baby *must* come first—even before her own needs. Otherwise she would blame herself for whatever happened in the future. She retorted, "You don't care a thing about me. Your're just interested in Tina!" I knew enough not to take this personally, and replied, "I'm interested in you both, and you know it, Alice. But Tina is my first priority and some day you'll be glad of it." I heard her sigh deeply at the other end before she hung up.

      This is another in what will be a long series of episodes for any single parent. Most have times when they feel as if life isn't fair and as if they are being pushed unfairly to give, give, give. The truth is, raising a small child is not at all easy—even if you are not alone. Alone, it becomes almost intolerable at times. But this is the time to be sure you are thinking of the baby's needs first. Regrets won't help later.

Alice needs a meaningful outlet for some of these feelings. If not a partner, she needs someone to unload on, someone to see her side with her. As a pediatrician, I remain the baby's advocate. Fortunately, the rewards are there, too, and these waves of stress do pass.

The next time I saw Alice was when she brought Tina in to my office with her first fever and respiratory infection. When I had diagnosed her and suggested treatment, Alice said, "Well, I guess this is my fault. If I didn't have to leave her with those runny-nosed kids, she wouldn't have to get these things." I said, "I guess you're bound to take anything that happens to her as your personal responsibility. But all children get colds and they need to build up an immune system to help control them. Tina will need hers earlier, that's all. Alice retorted, "Well at least I'm at her beck and call, so you—and I—can't blame these colds on neglect!"

      Her anger at being presssed by her dual career is inevitable and understandable. She can use that anger as energy to help her meet the stress of working and mothering alone, just as long as she doesn't take it out on Tina.

7

The McNamaras

Back to Work

The baby had just begun to seem like a person by the time Ann had to return to work. The six weeks they had given her was all she dared take. She called a friend at the office to see whether she dared try for two more weeks, but her friend warned her that their boss was pretty uptight and was talking about cutting out "certain jobs." She thought that Ann had better come back on schedule. Ann was terrified of losing her job. She and John had barely been able to make ends meet with one child. Now, with two, what would happen? If Ann lost her job, they would really be in trouble.

Three-year-old Danny was having a pretty rough time of it at day care. His teacher told Ann he spent most of the day sitting in the corner, sucking his thumb. He participated with the other children only when pressed to do so. Ann thought he might still be depressed about the new baby. The teacher asked the Mc-Namaras to pay some extra attention to him to help him over this period of stress. When Ann discussed it with John, he lost his usual patience. "How can I do any more than I'm doing? Of course he's having a rough time. We all are. A new baby is what we didn't need!"

Some days, Ann felt so sad about Danny that she kept him home with her. He would nestle in next to her whenever she sat down, sucking his thumb and looking at her with wide, hungry eyes. He seemed to perk up when his father was home, and when she praised him for helping her, but she still felt as if she were failing him.

Timothy, the new baby, was no trouble. He simply slept and ate, and as a result, Ann tended to forget him. She left him in the bedroom most of the day, bringing him out into the living room just long enough to give him a bottle. He seemed to eat all right, and she was pretty sure he was gaining. But, at the end of the first month, she had no real impression of him—except as an added burden to an already overloaded household. The three rooms seemed full of clothes, beds, and people. Although she tried desperately to repress it, she couldn't help but wonder what lay ahead for them. Would the pressure let up?

Breast-feeding would have created more of a bond between Ann and Tim. But she felt she could not start it. She had to go back to work and knew she had better save all the strength she could for her "two jobs." Anyway, she thought of breast-feeding as a bit too intimate. If you are going to leave your baby to go to work, you can't get too intimate with him. It would lead him to expect more than he would get out of life. Besides, it would be too hard on her to give it up.

&. *I am convinced that many working parents guard themselves against an intimacy with their children that might cause pain when they return to work. John is away on two jobs, six days a week, ten to twelve hours a day. How does he dare consider real intimacy with his boys? And Ann may be seeing herself as a workhorse first and a mother second. We must reverse some of these values if we want children and family to become of primary importance. But how? Working is something the McNamaras have to do. They are too proud and principled to accept welfare. To these caring, admirable young people, welfare is, correctly so, a last resort. Our welfare programs require that applicants be "deficient." They must label themselves "needy" or "out of work" before they can get help. What does this kind of admission of failure do to one's self-image? How can we begin to create more incentive to struggle for the good of the family? Our welfare society tells young couples like the McNamaras, "It's better to give up" or "You're irresponsible to want another child, and you probably can't make it, anyway." They hear this at a time when they need reassurance and support. One obvious reaction is to resent the baby, to pass on to him the feeling that he's a burden and already a failure. We Americans can't afford to do this any longer!*

Because the day-care center would not take Tim until he was four months old, Ann called her mother for help. Her mother's job and responsibilities at home were heavy, too, and she just couldn't come to help Ann out. She suggested that Ann's aunt might help with the new baby. She was caring for her own grandchildren, who were two and four, at home. Could they offer her something to cover the baby's expenses? Could they get Tim to and from her house? It was thirty minutes by subway, but Ann felt she had no choice. Her mother's sister was not her first choice, but she was there and would at least take good physical care of the baby—if she would do it at all. Ann felt as if she were begging for a big favor. She would rather be able to choose the best place for her precious charge.

Ann's aunt greeted her. "I thought you'd be calling me before long. I knew that baby would be too hard for you." She began to complain about how hard her own life was, and only brightened when Ann offered her $100. a month for taking care of baby Tim—plus a supply of food and diapers.

&. *It must be very hard to have to barter with your child's future. Nowhere is the gap between social classes as obvious as in the kinds of provisions our society has made for the infants of middle and working classes. Good care is hard to find at any amount of money, but those who can pay have a choice. The more marginal working class family has to take what they can get. This usually means a caregiver who, inadequately paid and trained, resents her job and the babies, who are usually parked in front of a TV set. What kind of start is that for the baby—and for the family?*

A Relentless Schedule

Ann's day began at dawn. She had to get up in time to feed both boys, take Tim to her aunt's, take Danny to day care, and get to her office on time. This meant getting Tim's food and clothes for the day ready, preparing for the supper they would have that night. By the time she got to work, she had had a full day already, and had no time to worry about herself, to be exhausted, or to feel blue. It left her little time to think about her two boys' adjustment—and this was particularly painful. She spent most of the day worrying about them—her mind was only half on her work. She wondered if there were any way she could help them more. She longed for a time to sit down and hold baby Tim. She needed time to cuddle Danny. The luxury of being a family together seemed to be reserved for Saturdays. But by the time Saturday rolled around, there was so much to do around the house that she had little time for the children then either. She needed to plan for the whole week—to prepare meals, to shop ahead, to clean the house, to do the washing, and then to try to be with her children. Everything seemed to conspire against their time together. Her mother had a suggestion. Why not set up a rigid schedule for yourself on the weekends, as rigid as the one during the week? Plan a half-hour with Tim every four hours, an hour with Danny, morning and late afternoon, an hour with each other at the end of the day. The rest of the time she could portion out to the various chores. This made Ann groan even more. What worse fate than to have the weekends regimented just like the weekdays? It made it seem like life was just one long job—a sequence of duties that never ended. She began to feel more depressed.

The children came to her rescue. Danny, so glad to be with his mother on the weekends, seemed to sense her needs and began to perk up. He even tried to make jokes for her, perform, and make her laugh. She was grateful for his sensitivity and responded to his efforts. The baby began to smile and gurgle when she played with him. He seemed so responsive to her playful games that she began to show Dan how to play with "his baby." Soon Daniel could get Tim to laugh better than anyone else.

It is always fascinating and rewarding to me to see how responsive small babies are to just-older siblings. They seem particularly "hooked" on children's behavior, as if they can get in tune with it more easily than they can with adult behavior. This certainly helps with sibling rivalry.

Ann began to see that she could do a minimum of housework and get by. If she saved most of her time to be with and to attend to her boys, the payoff was enormous. It worked best if she started each part of their day by being solely with and for them, postponing housework until they were playing, satisfied, or asleep. The children seemed to need her full attention for a little while, then she could be available partway. But if she tried to do her work first, then go to them, it failed. She realized what "quality time" with her children meant. It meant paying complete attention to their needs, getting on their wavelength, and filling up their initial neediness. Then they could share her with her chores. In fact, they could play along beside her as she worked. From time to time, their need for her would build up again, and they would fuss or fall apart. If she stopped at that point, to pick them up and to love them, the crisis would resolve itself and she could go on. She began to learn each boy's rhythm for needing her and could almost anticipate it. The weekends began to improve.

John needed help adjusting to the new family. He worked such long hours and was so tired when he got home that it took a real surge of energy to make himself available to his family. Ann had to shut out her need for him, but wanted him to save some part of himself for the boys. She fed John at night, sat him down with a beer, and brought each child to him. It seemed pretty artificial, and she had to manipulate their times with their father carefully so that each child didn't fall apart at just the moment he was available. But when it worked, John relaxed and began to enjoy his two boys. On the weekends, he began to save a special time to be with each one, at her urgent suggestion.

🍂 *Is it part of Ann's nurturing role to set up their family life so carefully? Should John do more planning himself? In traditional families like the McNamaras, the expectation is that the mother is the one who is responsible for everyone's well-being—no matter how many roles she has to play. Ann's satisfaction will have to come from seeing it work. John already feels pressed to the wall, and it is very important to these little boys that he develop a positive relationship with them now. Ann is wise to take this responsibility, whether there is equal sharing or not.*

Day Care Problems

When the baby reached four months of age, Daniel's day-care center took them both. Ann was relieved to save the hour of subway rides, and her aunt was quite relieved to be unburdened. She knew the center had an infant room, but she had never seen it. Daniel's three-year-old class seemed okay, and he was happier there now.

Daniel was delighted that his brother could come to his school. When Ann took them over the first day, she noticed that Tim's room was dark and that only one person was in charge. Eight cribs lined the walls. Babies of different ages were in the cribs. They all turned to watch her as she brought Tim in. This was not what she had been promised. She had hoped she could go over Tim's day with the woman in charge, but the woman seemed so rushed, so busy changing diapers, that Ann finally left Tim and hurried off to work.

🍂 *Day-care personnel should respect the anguish of separation that any caring mother feels when she leaves her small baby with them. They should encourage her to talk about his schedule, what she would plan for his day if she could, and even to give them instructions. It would be her way of staying in touch with her baby. Ann should have sensed that something was wrong when the caregiver in the infants' room had no time for her. The demands on working women are so overwhelming, and their attempts to stay in touch with their baby so often poorly rewarded, that many working mothers resign themselves to a kind of abdication of responsibility. This is not good for the mother–infant relationship in the long run. Day-care personnel must be sensitive to this. The fact that there were eight babies to one worker worried Ann, but her sense of powerlessness clouded her vision.*

The caregiver continued to avoid Ann. After the first week spent trying to make contact with the worker, Ann began to feel very uncomfortable. Although the woman always seemed to be changing diapers, yet Timothy's bottom was raw from unchanged diapers. He grew quieter and quieter. When Ann brought him home, he began to avert his eyes from her overwhelming greetings at night. She tried to play with him on the way home, but he seemed easily fatigued. When Daniel talked too loud or jumped up and down, she noticed that Tim would wince, frown, and turn toward the wall. Each day he seemed a bit more sensitive and easily overwhelmed. He began to look pale and ate rather half-heartedly. She tried to talk to him at feeding times, but he would frown, withdraw from her gaze, and throw up his feeding if she persisted. Her inclination was to leave him in his room, because he seemed so overly sensitive to family noise. If she tried to play with him, he put his thumb in his mouth, shielded his eyes with the other hand, and tried to turn away from her. She blamed this behavior on the fact that he was making a big adjustment to his new situation. But, as each day passed, he grew worse, less reachable, more easily overwhelmed, and sadder looking. Ann was frightened. Tim only ate half his formula—he had eaten well two weeks before. She wondered whether he was ill.

A Depressed Baby

When John came home, he assured Ann that two weeks' poor eating wouldn't hurt the baby. But Ann worried more, and took Tim to their health station nearby. Not only had he not gained weight, but had lost six ounces. She asked the nurse practitioner whether there could be anything wrong. The nurse asked to have the pediatrician examine him. Both took Tim's appearance se-riously and ordered blood tests, which were normal. They found nothing physically wrong, but they too thought he looked de-pressed. As they reviewed his history with Ann, they heard about her concerns about the day-care center. They felt that this might be the key to this baby's "depression."

    A baby can become depressed just like an adult. When a baby's personality changes drastically, when he begins to avoid interpersonal contact rather than search for it, when he shows a kind of hypersensitivity to sounds, faces, and interac-tions, it could be a sign that his environment is not caring enough. A baby who also loses weight is classified as "failing to thrive." This is a syndrome which afflicts understimulated ba-bies, deprived of interpersonal stimulation, or sometimes over-stimulated ones. Either Tim is not getting the attention he needs, or it is in a form that is overwhelming for him. We see babies like this in nurseries where no one has time to understand and relate to each baby as an individual. René Spitz described this in orphanages where babies lay around without any interper-sonal attention except at feeding time. He called this an "ana-clitic depression," in which the babies withdrew from the world, no longer expecting any of the attention they need to thrive. They not only stop gaining weight, but begin to lose in spite of adequate calories. Their bodies no longer utilize food properly. Their immune systems are finally affected, and many of these institutionalized babies die of simple, concurrent infections which would not have overwhelmed them had they been thriving.

    How could Timmy have gone downhill so quickly? At his age, there are few ways a baby can handle an environment that does not nurture him. He can protest—crying a great deal for what he wants and misses. When this doesn't work, he may begin to give up. We see babies turn their faces to the wall if they are hospitalized and are not receiving enough nurturant care. Then, the final stage of adaptation to this deprivation is to turn inward and to restrict all outward reactions, just to exist in a vegetable state. This is the most severe form of depression. Tim must have been left alone most of the day. Because it was such a contrast to his earlier environment and to the one at home, it affected him deeply.

Taking Action

Ann, frightened and angry, no longer felt helpless. She wanted to find out for herself what Tim's world at day care was like. She asked for an emergency day off from work and went over to the center several times during the day. On no occasion did she see anything happening to the babies. Lying in their cribs, they stared at the ceiling or, propped up, watched the one source of stimulation—a blaring TV set. In front of it sat the overworked woman in charge of the infants, perfunctorily feeding one baby after another. She rarely looked down at them and never talked or played with them. No baby ever reached up to stroke her face or to explore her mouth while she held it in her arms to feed. They no longer expected her to react, for she was as depressed as they were. Ann looked around the room and tried to institute interactions with the other seven infants, but she got the same response from them that she got from Tim. Each baby, looking dazed, overwhelmed, turned away from her. Only one curly-headed little girl mustered up a weak smile for Ann.

Ann was horrified by what she had found. Her first inclination was to march into the director's office and complain. Then she realized that, as a working parent, she would be labeled a "crank" and asked to take her children elsewhere. She felt a responsibility to the other seven babies and their parents, who perhaps were as naive as she had been to let this condition go on. She also thought of Danny and decided to see if the rest of the center was as inadequate as the babies' room. Then she would find out how to round up the other parents for a more effective protest.

The other rooms were very different. The toddler room was gay, fun. The twelve toddlers, laughing noisily, were playing ring-around-the-rosy with the three caretakers. Next, Ann entered Daniel's room. It, too, seemed happy and cheerful. There were two groups of three-year-olds, of fourteen children each. Two older teachers and three helpers seemed to be making life exciting for the children. Each of the helpers had favorites with whom they played. Ann was relieved to see Daniel in the midst of one active group. One child stood sadly in a corner, by herself. Ann watched one of the helpers and two children try to break through the child's isolation. In the second room, two little girls off together seemed to shun the noisy large group. One teacher had her eye on these two and asked them from time to time if they were ready to join the others. Ann sensed the entirely different atmosphere in these rooms where the children were involved and excited with each other and with their play. Ann wanted to join them. Here adults were protecting the individualities of the children. These rooms lacked the withdrawn, depressed atmosphere of the babies' room.

Ann was so concerned about the babies' room that she found new resources and abilities within herself. She decided to try to find out what could be done, before stirring up the other parents. She knew that several things were wrong with the infant room: (1) it was understaffed, (2) the woman there was depressed and unresponsive to the babies, and (3) there was no real planning or curriculum for these babies. Ann went to the director. She had decided that to be aggressive would make the woman angry, defensive, so she tried to be calm, matter-of-fact.

First she praised the older rooms she had visited. As she did, she talked about how well staffed and individualized they were. She told how grateful she was for their care of Daniel. It was so hard to leave him and Tim, so she felt extra gratitude for such a caring place as the center.

Then she asked whether the director was worried about the ratio of adults to babies in the infant room. The director replied in an unexpected flood of words. "We just can't get anyone for that baby room! We can't afford to pay anything, and no one we can find will take such a terrible job. It's so unrewarding to feed and change babies. Anyway, I'm sure this doesn't pertain to you, but why would any mother leave a baby to work, unless she were literally starving. I'm afraid that most people I might hire feel that mothers ought to be home taking care of their own babies. This poor woman has to work; her husband is dying. So I'm afraid we got her for a bargain, but she has eight babies to tend to, poor soul. I know she's depressed, but I guess the babies can't tell. She didn't work out with the older kids. They didn't like her, so we moved her to the babies' room. I wish we had another person in there at least, so the babies could get out of their cribs and play a bit more. But, we do the best we can with what we've got."

    ❧ *This kind of prejudice about working mothers, usually less conscious than this, affects the care that babies get. "The babies can't tell" is such a dangerous and outdated idea that it makes you wonder about the judgment of the director. But the reward system—that is, the money and prestige involved—is so low that few high-calibre people go into day-care. This needs to change, if we want to protect the future development of our babies. An underpaid, overworked adult is in no condition to offer babies what they need. This is a critical period in which babies learn interaction patterns and develop "basic trust" for their future cognitive and emotional growth. A baby who remains as deprived as Tim is now could always be fragile in his social development.*

Ann left the director's office determined to get action. She felt a sense of conviction and assertiveness that was new to her. She got hold of a list of the parents and went to Daniel's teacher, whom she respected. She wanted to test out her plan on a sympathetic person who knew the center. When Ann explained what was happening in the infant room, Dan's teacher looked appropriately upset. She, to, felt something should be done. Ann said, "If it's a matter of money and of finding another person to hire, why not turn to the parents? We certainly can't afford to pay any more than we have to, but we can't leave Timmy here the way things are. If all the parents met together, do you think the director would let us help? She seems to have given up on that room." The teacher thought it might work and encouraged Ann to call a meeting of the parents. She promised to explain it to the other teachers and to the director.

Ann called each parent on her list and asked whether they had been worried lately about their baby's behavior. The parents were surprised. Their responses varied: "I thought she was just growing up and getting quieter." "It was a relief to have him quiet down. He'd been a bear when he first came home." They all said that they' could not survive without the center, and felt powerless to change anything. Most of them didn't want to "rock the boat" for fear the center would close the baby room. "Then what would we do?"

Ann suggested that they meet with the director and the teachers—"Not to complain, but to figure out together what to do." Some were enthusiastic; others, resigned. This frightened Ann.

She felt no sense of solidarity nor even any understanding about the implications of this for their babies.

Even John suggested that she was stirring up a hornet's nest. The next thing they knew, they'd be out on their ear. Ann felt frightened, but she was too worried about Tim to let it lie without a fight. Meanwhile, she redoubled her efforts with Timothy. She learned how to tell when he felt overwhelmed by her, as well as when he was able to respond. If she rocked him gently, singing to him in a low voice without looking at him, he relaxed and enjoyed it. If she was too vigorous, or if she looked at him while she sang, he would stiffen, then turn away. When he had had enough, he yawned, hiccoughed, his arms and legs went limp, and he arched his head and face away from her. Each day she could do a bit more and he began to look better. His color returned, his smile came gently back, and he began again to look at her and turn to listen to his brother. He was beginning to regain his vigor and interest at home.

🐚 *We have learned from our work with premature infants and sick, fragile babies that it is easy to overload them with too much or too vigorous stimulation. They give clues when they have had enough. One type of approach at a time works—either touch, voice, look, or rocking—but not more than one. A low-keyed pace is more likely to reach these babies. Too much at once may make them turn off or spit up. To us, this represents a nervous system that is fragile but still open to information for learning. The baby can only handle new experience at his own rate, if it is to be positive. The intestinal tract, heart, lungs, and nervous system are all easily overwhelmed in a depressed and understimulated baby. It is a testimony to the resiliency of the human organism that a baby like Tim can recover so readily, and a testimony to Ann's empathy and mothering skills that she recognized his needs.*

The meeting of the parents and staff could have been a disaster. The staff seemed to be on the defensive. Ann played the role of spokesperson. She said that she knew they all wanted the same thing for the children. She really appreciated what the staff did and how demanding a job it was. The older children were so happy and thriving at the center, but the babies' room seemed to lack support from parents. Could they help locate a second trained, sensitive person and participate themselves? Could each couple participate half a day? She and John would come in a half-day each. It meant making some sort of trade-off with the bank where she worked, but she was willing to risk it. Several families finally agreed. Then one of the teachers in the older group suggested that they have a consultant in to design a curriculum for these small babies. She quoted Bruno Bettelheim, "Love is not enough," and said that a more dependable structure was needed. Ann then pointed out that two paid people meant more fees from each family, unless there was some way of getting a subsidy from an outside source. Did the director have any ideas? Everyone's help was needed in this project, but weren't the babies worth it? So convincing was her speech that the staff clapped and the parents began to feel empowered. The meeting came to an end as they all made plans to help. Ann felt that she had somehow learned something new about herself in this crisis.

The director of the center stood up. "This is just the kind of help we need from you parents. Mrs. McNamara came in to observe our baby room, and she saw the problems we face. We need more help, more money, and we do need you all to participate. I've figured out that we can share part of the costs all over the center. In the baby room, we'll need $10 each more a week, but maybe I can find that somewhere else. If each parent can be there a half-day a week as a helper, we can get through, just until we get two good trained people, I guarantee." This turned out to be a real solution, and the babies' room quickly became a showplace. Another teacher had an idea about hiring a child development student from a local college, and the parents began to figure together how they could help. The staff and parents teamed up to work toward a mutual goal.

  One difficult thing in day care is keeping parents involved. Teachers get discouraged and turned off when parents are passive and distant. Competition between teachers and parents is inevitable, but can easily turn into exciting cooperation.

This meeting changed the tenor of the center. The infants' room began to gather so much interest that other families and teachers came in to see what was going on. Ann felt like a heroine.

Participating in Day Care

To her surprise, the bank was willing to give Ann a half-day off each week to be at the center. It was like a picnic. Not only could she devote herself to Timmy and two or three other babies, but also she could see Danny. He was so proud to have his mother at "his school." Ann sat with three babies in chairs around her to play with them. They joined in on her songs with squeals of their own, soon all four trilling along together. Then she gave them a toy to reach for and transfer, showing them how to hand it from one to another. Before long she had them interacting with each other. They watched Ann, watched each other, then giggled and cooed at each other, back and forth. The eight-month-olders on the floor crawled up to each other and felt each other's arms, face, and hair. Ann often had to extract their hands from a tight grip on each other's anatomy. As she watched, she realized how much pleasure she got out of observing and learning from them—in a situation free of other things to do. At nap time, or the end of a session, she had a chance to sit down with the teachers and discuss all the behavior and events she had been a part of. This chance to participate was becoming a rare sort of learning experience for Ann.

A Baby As a Person

Not long afterward Ann came in to leave Tim off for the first time with Mrs. Kahn, the new staff member in the infants' room. They sat down together. "Tell me all about Tim as a person. What is he like? When does he eat and sleep? What kinds of things does he play with?" Mrs. Kahn was ready, pencil poised, to take notes. Ann was caught off guard. She really hadn't even thought of Tim as a "person." She had been dealing with him as a "baby," answering his needs. She never really had the time—or the incentive—to think about him as anything but a baby.

&. *This is a serious problem in giving up a baby so soon. With so many pressures, Ann had no time to see Tim as an individual. Even though she probably sensed some special traits of his, she hadn't had the energy or time to concentrate on him in this way. Perhaps the fact that she would have to share him so soon had made her unconsciously wary of seeing him as a person who might have feelings about being left to another. Six weeks was not enough. If Ann could have had at least four months at home, she might have dared to get to know Tim, and to help Danny over his adjustment and back to school at his own time. If she could have gotten past the period of colic, of physical and psychological readjustment, the whole family would have had a better chance. If John could have afforded a leave to stay home for two months or so to get involved with his new family, what a different future they would have had.*

As she began to tell Mrs. Kahn all she could about Tim, tears welled up and her voice caught. She had guarded herself so well during the crisis that she had not realized the strength of her feelings. She began to talk about how sturdy and easy-going he was, how he liked his bottle right on time. Soon she was holding him tighter, wishing she knew him better. The teacher assured her that she would take very special care of him, and that he would be ready and waiting for her at the end of the day. Ann felt he was in good hands, but realized again that he had hardly been hers before she had to leave him. She looked back at her year at home after Dan came and wished she could have done as much for Tim.

That day at work seemed one of the longest of Ann's life. She wanted to phone the center every other minute, but she restrained herself. Finally, time came to go get her two boys. She fumbled with her coat, and had a hard time finding the token for the bus. She thought the bus driver would never get through the traffic. When she finally got to the center, she rushed in to Danny first. He clung to her, and said, "I missed you. Where were you?" She explained that she was just late from work, but she could see that Danny's mind was elsewhere. He had been afraid that she had taken off with the baby. When she finally realized this and explained that she wasn't with the baby either, he said, "I knew you weren't. I went to see Timmy." His teacher told Ann that he had wanted to check up on Tim and had been taken to see him. She had commended Danny on being so protective of Tim. Ann knew that his protectiveness covered up his real concern—that Tim might go home with his mother, without Danny.

When they picked up Tim in the baby room, she had the presence of mind to give him to Danny to hold first. Then she hugged both boys and said, "Now we are all together again!" Dan wriggled out of her arms, off to play, and she had a moment to hug her baby. He seemed quiet to her, and she found herself looking for things that might be wrong with him. Mrs. Kahn assured her that he had been an angel, hadn't fussed, and had finished all his bottles. Ann wondered whether Mrs. Kahn would tell her if anything had gone wrong.

* When Mrs. Kahn said Tim was "an angel," Ann wonders whether she is just being reassuring. The truth is that babies clearly recognize differences in caregivers by four to six weeks. With Ann's sensitivity to his depression, and Mrs. Kahn's more motivated approach, Tim is probably going to thrive again.*

The End of the Day

Ann barely got both babies on the bus home before they began to break up. Dan was negative, sulky, impossible. Timmy seemed alternately limp one moment and fussy the next. She literally fell in the front door. Both babies began to cry. Danny for her attention; Timmy to be fed. She began to weep herself, and Danny stopped to watch her in dismay. Then he went to the refrigerator and pulled out one of Timmy's bottles. With that, Ann sat down in a big rocking chair, pulled Danny up into her lap, and hugged him. He clung to her, and she just sat with her two babies in her lap rocking and rocking. As they rocked, she began to feed Timmy the bottle. It was cold, but he gulped it down, and she began to feel at peace again. As she pulled herself together, Dan and Tim both began to settle down to a lovely, cozy time.

≈ *The real trouble with having to work all day is that there's not enough energy left over. Ann must feel pretty empty and washed out by the end of the day. Trying to make up to the children for the day away from home takes a lot of stamina. Dan saved her this time by his helpful gesture. She needed a bit of mothering herself. It is easier when a father can be home to help the family over some of these rough transitions. As time goes on, she will have to learn to pace herself—to save enough of herself to make up to the children for her absence all day. Even though a child can adjust to a day-care or play school situation, it really isn't likely to compare, in his mind, with being home with his parent. So, the end of the day needs to be a time of reunion and restitution—for all of them.*

One evening, a few weeks later, Ann had them all quieted down and was in the process of feeding Dan, when Tim began to whimper. She rushed to him to see what was wrong. She diapered him, offered him more food, but he turned way. She couldn't stand to hear him cry, and she frantically searched for the reason. She had forgotten that he had had a regular fussy period every evening and that this crying was probably a part of that.

≈ *Every imperfection, every untoward event, looms large if a mother has had to leave her baby all day. I'm sure it's a combination of feeling guilty at having been away, at a loss as to what went on at day-care that she doesn't know about and can't control, and a real longing to be of use to the baby all over again. So Ann's rather hectic search for what was making Tim cry is part of her own attempt to get back into the role of being his mother and being needed by him.*

She found that, when she carried him around, he was perfectly happy. Her mother had given her a carrier that kept Tim up next to her chest. She put him in it and went about the business of getting Dan's supper and her own. This certainly seemed to be the answer to Tim's woes, for he was wide awake, looking at her as she worked. Whenever she glanced down at him, he smiled and wriggled. When he tried to make a sound, she could reinforce it with an imitation of her own. She had never seen him so communicative.

      This is another example of how a baby saves up his important communications for his mother.

Ann felt they were back on track with each other and that Timmy had really done it. After she got Dan's supper going, she sat at the table with the two of them, feeling at peace with the world.

But that night, Tim began to cry again, inconsolably, for about an hour. Ann felt desperate. Her mother called to see how she was faring at the end of her first working day. She told her mother about Timmy's crying, and her mother reminded her that this was not necessarily the result of having been left in day care. He had been fussy back during the two weeks she was there. Like magic, this reassurance lifted the burden of self-blame, and Ann could see that this was not a new, or even an unexpected, part of Tim's day.

      When a mother has to leave a small baby, every event seems to call up her guilt, her feeling that she is responsible for anything even remotely harmful to the baby. She is likely to lose sight of the normal developmental processes as she blames herself.

As soon as she calmed down, Timmy did, too. And after his fussy period was over, he went right to bed and slept well. She had time to read to Dan, to comfort him, and to get him to bed without the baby between them.

When she finally got a chance to think about feeding herself, she was too exhausted, and fell gratefully into bed at nine o'-clock. She never even heard the phone ring. John was trying to call her from a nearby town. After a long ring, he realized that she was probably sound asleep. He had to suppress his own wish to be there to help her. He never had much of a family life of his own, and he longed to be there now.

8
Evaluating Day Care

There are so many things to consider when faced with leaving a precious baby in another's care. The fact that it is so painful makes it even harder to make clear, objective decisions.

Substitute Care at Home

The ideal situation in many cases might be a paid sitter at home. For a small baby, having only one environment to learn about may be easiest. Familiar cues are coupled with less disruption. Each day the baby learns a single routine. But such caregivers are expensive, often unavailable, untrained and their motives may not be clear. Stories of caregivers parking babies in front of television sets in order to be able to go about their own business are all too familiar. There is also a danger of "burnout," or too many different caregivers. I often recommend to mothers that they look for a caregiver who has a reason of her own for wanting to take care of another person's baby. Perhaps she has a baby of her own or some other personal reason for being at home. She should be both nurturant and intelligent. *Always* check references. In addition, go home at unannounced times during the day to check up on what's happening. Always have a reason so the caregiver won't feel she's being watched. It is critical that you know what kind of care your baby is getting. If you don't, you will be more competitive and hovering than if you do.

As I have pointed out several times, competition with a caregiver is inevitable for a caring parent. You are bound to resent sharing your baby, and your feelings will come out in unexpected, unconscious ways. Everything a caregiver does for your baby will be, for you, just a little bit wrong. She may carry your baby awkwardly, or bathe her too sloppily. Or she will discipline your child when you wouldn't. Or she'll leave dirty clothes around. Unless her habits are dangerous to the baby, I urge you not to bring them up. Anyone who cares about your baby will also feel unconscious competition and resentment toward you. She may even feel that you aren't so great for the baby, either, and that she needs to cushion your baby against your childrearing practices. She may feel you are too lazy and are spoiling your baby. This competition is the same as that which springs up between father and mother. In other words, it is normal and inevitable. Don't let it come between you and the caregiver.

If you are looking for a person to be at home with your baby, watch to see whether or not she respects the child's personality (Does she wait until the child is ready to make an advance?) and his or her stage of development (Does she talk baby talk when the child is already older?). Does the person understand your child's needs (Does she answer her questions as if she respected them? Does she pick her up to comfort her when she needs it? Does she acknowledge a bid for attention?)? At Children's Hospital, some house officers put their hand on top of the child's hand when the child tries to interrupt a conversation with the mother. A caring adult needn't stop talking, but he or she does need to acknowledge a child's urgent bid for attention.

Last of all, does the substitute caregiver appeal to you? Is she aware and respectful of your needs in separating from your baby? Will she listen to you when you try to tell her what you went through last night? Is she willing to discuss structuring the day, perhaps with an afternoon nap, so that the baby will be ready for you when you return at the end of the day? You need to have a time with your baby in which he or she is fresh and receptive. "Quality time" should be a reward for both of you. If your baby is exhausted, frazzled at the end of the day, all of your own resolve to save up time and energy for her will have been in vain. I remember one mother's comment when I asked her about her sitter. She said admiringly, "She's the kind of generous lady who says to me 'She may be about to take her first step any time. I hope it will be for you.' I know my baby has already taken her first step while I was away, but I wanted to be there for it and this woman knew it. So when my baby does take a step, I have a chance to think of it as mine!"

If your sitter is in too big a hurry to leave at the end of the day and hasn't enough time to tell you what has been going on all day, watch out! I would want someone who describes your baby's accomplishments with the same enthusiasm you do. If she can describe the *way* your baby learned a new task, you can be pretty sure she's deeply involved and has identified with your baby.

Whether or not you and the substitute caregiver do things the same way isn't necessarily critical, from the baby's standpoint. A baby can adjust to two very different caregivers—just as she can to two very different parents. She will learn very quickly how to save for you the behavior that is appropriate to you and for your substitute, that which is appropriate for her. I always feel that parents don't need to agree on behaving alike with their baby. It's not even possible, and the child all too quickly senses the dishonesty. The same is true with a sitter. But you do need to be sure that you and she are in enough agreement so that you don't undermine each other's work with the child. That will indirectly undermine the child's faith in each of you.

Family Day Care

In this second alternative, the mother of a child takes several others into her own home. It is usually less expensive than a single sitter. It is also possible to check up on the situation a bit more carefully by calling the other families who leave their children with the family day-care person. There is still another advantage. Your child will have other children around to play with. By the end of the first year, this is very important. The second year is a time for real learning from each other—by imitation, by parallel play, and so on. Chances for excitement without boredom are greater. If the family day-care person can tolerate several children and at the same time be sensitive to each one's needs, it is the best way to provide care for your child.

Discuss the situation with the other parents. Try to be there for special events in the day—such as parents' leavetaking in the morning or reunions at night. At those times, you can tell how sensitive the secondary caregiver is to your child and to the particular parents' issues involved in leaving and returning. I would never leave my child in the hands of someone who literally shoos me out or doesn't let me separate gradually from my child. Also, I would want to be sure she makes herself available to the distressed child who is being left, and in an appropriate way for that child. Mealtimes or crises are also events that can be very revealing. Is the caregiver sensitive to each child's particular level of development? Does she allow a ten-month-old time to finger-feed, a toddler to smear food? Since your baby is bound to make a fuss when you leave each day, you can't be sure that he or she is getting along with the new caregiver, unless you sneak back a little later. But don't let your baby see you, unless you are prepared to stay for awhile. It's too much to ask your child to adjust to your leaving twice.

Day-Care Centers

Choosing a center where you can leave your child is likely to be a real wrench for you. How can you feel comfortable about the prospect? No matter how urgent it is that you go back to work, either for financial or for career reasons, it is difficult to be objective about taking a small child away from the comfort and familiarity of home.

However, in a good day-care center, there are many opportunities for you and for the child. Your child will have playmates, and you and your spouse will have a chance to form relationships with other working families. These can be very rewarding.

Relationships between working families that revolve around a center make the center a community that replaces some of what we lose by giving up an extended family life. With this concept in mind, there are movements that cement peer families, elderly groups, and young children who are not related but who become included in such centers as if they were. The benefits for the three generations are obvious. They surmount the interpersonal pressures that have been driving generations of families apart. The opportunities to reinforce good childrearing practices, to model and teach strengths to the child and to parents under stress, are also great in centers where these are priorities.

The standards I look for first of all are (1) safety and cleanliness; (2) caregivers who are well trained, who like babies, and who are willing to treat them as individuals; (3) caregivers who know what babies need in the way of stimulating experiences and opportunities for learning about themselves and their world; and (4) staff who are flexible and prepared to adjust to the sleep and waking rhythms of each baby. This last is a window to the quality of caring. Nutrition, safety, and attention to illness all seemed to correlate with this in a study we recently made at Boston Children's Hospital.

Health and safety issues are of course, *critical*. Look for uncovered light sockets, unprotected "traps," medicines within reach, and unprotected detergents in the kitchen.

Most important of all are the human relationships in the program. Do people seem to like and respect each other? Do you feel that you are a member of the team, or do you feel defensive while you're there? Do they encourage relationships and group settings with other parents?

What is the turnover rate in the center? Do people who work there seem happy? Have they outlets for their frustrations and their questions?

I always want to be sure that the workers are well trained and relatively well paid. These are the conditions for quality care. If we continue to allow centers to hire untrained, poorly paid workers, children are bound to suffer. Having a good heart is not enough for a caregiver. There are too many conflicting demands from so many children during a day in a center. Sooner or later, the demands exceed one's patience. An untrained worker is less likely to have the knowledge necessary to handle his or her own frustrations as well as the babies' demands. Abuse or neglect of a particularly demanding child could be the result.

Some good questions you can ask yourself as you look for good day-care for your baby are suggested by Ellen Galinsky and W. A. Hooks in a book called *The New Extended Family* (see the References):

Would you want to spend the day here with this person (or persons)?

What happens when a visitor enters the room? Do all the children look up, hungry for a new face, some excitement? Or do they look up briefly, then return to what they are doing, as if it were more critical?

Do the caregivers pay attention to parents at arrival and discharge, allowing them time to express their concerns—or are they glad to see them go? Do they give the child enough time and attention to soften the pain of separation?

What are the transitions like? If the caregivers help a child make it from one activity to another with sensitivity, you are likely to be in good hands.

How does the staff handle mealtime? Are they sensitive to the child's need to experiment with food, to test out self-feeding, for extra attention at mealtime?

The recent publicity that has followed cases of sexual abuse in day-care centers is frightening working parents to death. How can they be sure their small child is safe from this kind of threat? I have discussed this with many parents. One way to be sure is to go to your child's center at unexpected times during the day to see what is going on. When I suggest this, parents say, "But they ask me to come only at special times. I wouldn't dare. They might take it out on my baby if I disobey their rules." I would question those rules. You have a right to be there, and a center that doesn't want you at all times is suspect. Since the publicity, any center should be eager to have loyal, participating parents involved, in order to prevent ungrounded accusations which might result in lawsuits.

How can you teach children to protect themselves without scaring them unnecessarily? There are some new studies investigating this, and no one yet has all the answers. But I would start early to assure three- and four-year-olds that their genitals are "their own" and are private. I would help them realize that if they don't want older people to touch or handle them, they should say so—and even cry about it. I respect this in my office, always asking for their permission to examine them. I never ask them to take their underpants completely off, "because that part of your body is special, and you might like to keep it covered." I have thought of trying to talk to them about grown-ups who are too intrusive, but I feel it is really the parent's role. Hence, I encourage parents to be conscious of this need to explain the specialness of their bodies to small children.

I am not sure yet how to pass on to children the fact that there are certain kinds of adults whom you can't trust, without scaring them away from all strangers. You can certainly teach a child to say. "That's bad hugging. Let me go." or "Don't touch my genitals. They're mine." Perhaps a parent can point out that there are some adults who are too crazy or childish to be trusted as adults. One of my daughters was confronted, at the age of five, by such a person. She knew immediately he was "strange" and wanted to run away from him. She did so, and then told me about it as if she needed to be reassured that she was right in repudiating an adult. Of course, I could and did assure her, but I also told her how proud I was of her to talk to me about it. For I knew children may feel a certain kind of guilt and attraction to such an event, which might have made my daughter keep it to herself. If a parent can maintain an open relationship in which a child can talk about such things, the opportunity to help the child afterward can be significant. It is possible to do this, without an unnecessary emphasis on sexuality, if you are open in your relationship—and as early as possible.

There are many other issues that need to be addressed in providing good substitute care for your child. First of all, as I have pointed out, the ratio of adults to small children is critical. Four babies, or toddlers, to one adult is the upper limit. For very small babies, three to one is better. One adult to five children between two and five years old is another guideline. And, of course, anything you are able to learn about the training and experience of these adults is important. Do they understand the various developmental stages? Do they respect the child's individual rhythms and need for fantasy and play? One trend today bothers me. It is the feeling that we must teach small children to perform, to read, to write, as early as possible. Early learning is not the goal. Although it's perfectly possible to teach children to read and write much earlier than they do, they may lose out on other, more important, age-appropriate tasks, such as learning about each other and about how to handle themselves as people. Also, I have seen children who were taught to read and write early but who could not generalize this learning later on in childhood. In second and third grade, they began to fail because the learning techniques they used earlier no longer worked for complex learning.

Look hard for teachers and caregivers who are sensitive to the age levels and interests of the child in all areas at once—motor, social, cognitive. If the child is pushed too hard on one, he or she may perform, but at what cost to other lines of development? A center that respects play as a child's way of mastering his or her world would be my choice. Support and flexible availability of adults—to allow children to find their own way of learning—would be ideal. Children can be encouraged, without pushing, to learn adult tasks. Childhood is short enough and precious as a time for free exploration and experimentation. Cheating children of time to play and dream is a real danger these days. Look for teachers who are childlike themselves or who treasure the excitement of childhood.

Finally, I want to emphasize that parents should always look for caregivers who value the parents' own relationship with their child. If they can discuss that with you, or if they can help you acknowledge your feelings of loneliness and desertion at having to give up your child, they will be more ready to respect and support you from day to day. Whether at a day-care center or at home, I encourage you to look for caregivers who can care for you as well as for you child. And then I urge you to let them know how much you appreciate them and all they do for all of you as a family. If father and mother can applaud the sitter, or participate in the day-care center, their children will benefit.

PART III

Hurdles
For
Working
Parents

9

The Snows

⟨⟩ There are certain times when problems arise in working families. I have seen them repeatedly and can predict when and why they are likely to occur. Since they are predictable, and the forces that play into them are universal ones, we should be able to avoid or at least to mitigate them. They are concerned with a baby's spurts of development, or learning about independence. Since these are difficult times in any family and drain the resources even of families where one parent is at home, it is no surprise that they are even harder for dual-career couples. Parents with limited energy and time for their children are bound to be more stressed when the usual balances are not working. They are bound to feel angry and guilty that they are angry and that they haven't the energy to meet the emergency.

Development in small children progresses unevenly. When any one line (the motor, emotional, physical, or cognitive) takes a spurt, the others are left behind. All the child's energy is utilized in the new learning spurt—and all the family's resources will be called upon, too. The child will regress and be more demanding day and night. She will be dissatisfied with herself—and with

125

those around her. Her usual supports won't be enough. Her thumb or her blanket or her baby doll won't suffice. Even when you gather her up to love her and rock her, she may fall apart, and scream or cry inconsolably. You are not enough, either. Any caring parent inevitably feels it's his or her fault. What have I done? Or, Why can't I do the right thing to help? Working parents blame it on their situation. If they were there enough, if they were more available when they came home, and if they had had more energy for the child, this misery would never have occurred. I've seen very few working parents who can take these crises without feeling guilty and responsible. If a parent is at home all day, she (or he) is less likely to feel responsible, because she (or he) will have seen this pattern of disintegration before each new spurt in development. It represents an attempt on the child's part to muster an unusual amount of energy for an unusual task of learning. The disintegration and regression calls up an alarm energy from within which demands responsiveness from those around. This in turn energizes the child for the new spurt.

When the family is working, there is rarely enough energy left over for these extra demands. The parents feel too pressed and angered by the sudden changes in the child to understand what is happening. They attempt to pacify the child. Since pacification is not what she needs, the result is only a repetition of the demands. Parents become more upset and unable to tolerate the autonomy which might lead to a real resolution and spurt in development. A problem between them is hatching. In this chapter and the two that follow I emphasize some of these developmental hurdles so that stressed working parents can recognize them and avoid becoming locked in a struggle with their developing child.

Avoiding Eating Problems

All during the day at work Carla looked forward to her evening with Amy. She and Amy talked and gurgled. Amy tried to imitate Carla with the spoon and the cup. She played with the bits of food which Carla gave her to feed herself. It was a delightful time at the end of the day. Carla watched Amy use her newly developed pincer grasp and marveled at the delicacy of her fingers.

> *This emphasis on meals may be difficult when Amy hits a negative period and the feeding area becomes a provocative battleground. Carla, like many working mothers, is likely to feel especially responsible for keeping feedings happy and successful, since they symbolize a period of close communication after being away from each other all day. For this reason, feeding problems are more likely in working families, unless the parents recognize the forces behind negativism and their own urge to control the situation. Feeding and sleeping are two areas in which the development of independence in the child may be at cross purposes with the parents' needs to prolong dependence. Letting the baby become independent in this area as soon as possible is a safeguard against feeding problems in the second year. The excitement of newly found skills takes up a lot of energy that might otherwise be spent in negative behavior and teasing.*

As Amy picked up bits of food, smashing them in her fist and watching them squeeze out at the end of her hand, Carla winced. Then Amy ate the squeezed-out food off her hand and giggled, as if she knew it bothered her mother.

New Achievements

Amy began to exult in her fingers. She pointed to everything, saying "Dat," "Dis," all day long. When her parents arrived to pick her up at the end of the day, they were treated to an almost constant display of her new achievements. She poked into every nook and cranny. The electric sockets caught her interest. Carla and Jim might not have thought to search their house for "traps," if the day-care center hadn't alerted them. They were suddenly aware that they had been enjoying her development without realizing that each new step brought them a new responsibility.

≈ Working parents are likely to be away for the long, often tedious hours of a child's exploration with a newly acquired motor skill. At the center, the staff will have seen how Amy fills up the time, exploring, tasting, experimenting. The danger of her exploration is that she won't know where to stop. She will try to touch and taste everything—kettles, electric cords, poisons, plants. The Snows will only see the end of the day— when Amy will be showing off for them, and when there are plenty of adult eyes watching her. The long days of experimentation contain dangers they will learn about only on weekends.

Superbaby Syndrome

Jim began to teach her how to point to animals in a word book. "Where's the cat?" "Where's the dog?" Amy was so eager to please her father that she sat for long periods in his lap trying to learn to please him. After a few weeks, Amy could go through the whole picture book. She was beginning to try to imitate some of the words. She said, "Ca," "Do" in imitation of her father. He was so thrilled with "their" success that he began to try to teach her "one, two, three." She learned this, too. Jim bought a book called "How to Teach Your Baby to Read," and was about to go on, when Carla put her foot down. "Have fun, but don't get too serious. She falls apart after you are through."

≈ Small children are so eager to please a parent who is not there all day that they will make enormous efforts. Carla is right. Amy is putting all she can into living up to her father's wishes already. She lets herself be pushed to learn, but it isn't on her terms. She's doing it "for him." Over the years, many writers on child development have suggested that early teaching paves the way to later success in cognitive development. I do not agree. In the 1960s, two- and three-year-old children were taught to read and to type long words and sentences. I saw small children reading and typing words that seemed well beyond their age. Their strained little faces and worried expressions when they looked up for adult approval, their relieved smiles when they were correct and were rewarded—all of these

were evidence to me of the expense of these acquisitions. Such children did well in first grade, but began to lag in second and third. By third grade their earlier precocity was no longer panning out. The learning models they had acquired did not seem to generalize to the demands of learning later on. Meanwhile, their self-images had come to depend on adult approval. When they no longer got it, their fragility began to show. Precocity in a child often carries a cost with it—too often a cost in other developmental areas, such as social or emotional development.

In Jim's case, this desire to teach Amy to do learning tasks early is based on a combination of pride, awe at her ability to be coached, and delight in her wish to please him. All of these are understandable and rewarding to Amy as they are communicated to her. Of course, a working parent should find ways to communicate and play at the end of the day. Teaching words and numbers rewards them both. The danger is in getting carried away with one mode and excluding others. A parent who is around all day is likely to get a better sense of the balances in a child's life—between the cognitive, motor, and emotional lines of development. Pushing her in one area for a time will certainly not be a deficit, but she must learn in other areas also.

One reason that the "superbaby syndrome" has caught on readily in this generation is that there is a kind of vacuum in cultural values for young parents. Cognitive performance is easy to measure and to demonstrate to your friends. It becomes a way for young parents to feel successful in their parenting. Those of us who are more interested in social and emotional development for children haven't made the guideposts in these areas explicit enough for parents so they can see when they have done a good job. My own bias is strong. Emotional development is the base for future cognitive success. If a child develops a good sense of himself and of his competence in all areas, he will be ready to acquire cognitive competence later on. Motivation, prolonged attention to learning, and the joy of success will come easily at an appropriate time in his life. An emotionally fulfilled child will also have enough self-image to care about others and be ready to give to others as well as to acquire for himself. Our society may need a serious reevaluation—we are raising children to be highly individualistic, intellectually clever, and self-motivated—to the exclusion of caring about others around them. Do we want to create cognitive monsters?

Jim and Amy continued to have their time together at the end of the day, while Carla fixed supper. Jim's share was to clean up afterward while Carla bathed Amy and got her ready for bed. In this way, each of them had a special time with her. Each of them kept one ear cocked to see what the other was doing with Amy. When she was ready for bed, they all sat around together, cuddling and talking and reading. Amy knew this was "her" time and she played it for all she was worth. She'd snuggle into Jim's lap until her mother began to fidget, then she'd go cuddle with Carla. Back and forth she'd go, as if she knew how jealous they each were.

    This natural, inevitable jealousy over a first baby is a cementing force as well as a potentially splitting one, if Carla and Jim let it become a reason for battling. But if they can see Amy's testing of each of them as a way of gathering in all the loving she can get, they will avoid hostility with one another. A triangle is a very forceful enclosed entity, and the forces within it can be equal in all directions.

Illnesses

Amy began to have one cold after another. Every other week, she came down with a fresh cold. Carla caught it from her one week, Jim the next. It seemed as if they handed it back and forth from one to the other. At the beginning of each cold, one parent had to stay home. Again their lives were disrupted; Carla and Jim wondered how long their firms would put up with it. By now they had learned to share each day off so that each had only a half day's absence. But three days running with each cold every other week undermined their reliability at work. Carla also worried about Amy. Did these colds reflect her depression at being left in day care? Were they going to tear down Amy's health so that she would come down with a more serious illness? How long should she stay home with each cold? Were she and Jim sending Amy back to day care too soon, to serve their own purposes? All these questions ran through their heads.

    ❧ *Parents who place a small child in day care with other children need to be warned that their child will pick up one thing after another. Each infection goes the rounds of the entire center. Until each child has had enough respiratory infections to build up her general immunity, it is likely that she'll have one cold after another. I see this in a university community. As new children move into an area crowded with other children, they are bound to be sick over and over until they get immune to all the new germs. Then they'll be well for years to come—their immunity will be high. About every four or five years, they will have to go through a bad period again. Each cold is better handled without medication unless there is a complication. The longer a child can fight it, the more immunity will develop. Each bout of antibiotics will clean out her throat of normal, protective flora and she'll have to start over to recolonize it. The first few months in day care create an inevitable cycle of infections. Another part of the trouble is that a small child's germs are more virulent to adults than are other adults'. So parents are very likely to share their child's colds. Working parents need to plan for many absences at first, both to keep the child out long enough to recover, and to take care of themselves through this period.*

    One night Carla and Jim awakened with a start. Amy was crying with a cry they'd never heard before. She sounded really ill. They felt her forehead. She was burning up, and looked at them with glazed eyes. Her whole body was limp and trembling. She breathed rapidly and shallowly. When they took her temperature, it was 104° Fahrenheit. They could hardly believe it. They were sure she would die before they could help her. They had never heard of such a high fever. They rushed to call their pediatrician. He sounded as if he were asleep, and not very impressed with their report. He said wearily, "All small children have high fevers if they have one at all. Does she have any other things to go with the fever? The serious symptoms are easy to spot—either a stiff neck in which she can't bend her head forward on her chest, or she'll pull on a very sore ear, or she'll show you real trouble in breathing. Anything else can wait until the morning and we can tend to it then if we need to." Carla and Jim were concerned with her breathing. He said to try her on an aspirin substitute* (the dose was 1 grain per year) and to cool her off in a tub of lukewarm water if she was too miserable. Meanwhile, she needed clear fluids—not milk or water, but sugary or salty fluids such as broth, jello, ginger ale, sugar water, or very diluted, sweetened fruit juices. If, an hour after the aspirin substitute, she seemed better, that was a good sign. If she continued to look worse, it might be worth checking her out. But, in all likelihood, the fever was not serious and was just a sign of an infection she was fighting. Small children are likely to fight them with sudden high fevers at night, which come down before morning. If the fever is still there, it would be time then to check her out.

Both parents were as limp as Amy was. Though her doctor's words were reassuring, and they followed his suggestions, they could hardly believe that she wasn't terribly sick. When her fever went down an hour later, and she sat up in bed and began to play, it seemed like a miracle that she could improve so quickly.

      ❧ *Any new parent is overwhelmed by the first illness and by such a high fever. Nine out of ten of these will be simple viral infections. But the signs need to be heeded and learned. Any parent's immediate reaction is to feel guilty and responsible for the child's illness. Working parents may feel extra guilty and besieged. When they must blame it on her exposure to other children at day care, they feel an added responsibility. If they weren't working, she wouldn't need to be exposed so early.*

Jim and Carla stayed by Amy's bed all night, dozing fitfully. They didn't dare leave her. The next morning, she was better, but she still seemed more limp than usual. Carla checked with her office. She had an appointment she couldn't break. Jim felt trapped at having to be the one who stayed home. He, too, was anxious. Carla, what will I do if something happens to her? Suppose her fever shoots up?" He did not want to have total responsibility.

Amy's fever bounced up and down for the next three days before she finally began to get better. Her doctor looked her over

---

* Because of the association with a disease called Reye's Syndrome, aspirin is no longer recommended for children with high fevers.

when their anxiety could no longer be contained. He declared it to be a viral disease, roseola, and told them they would just have to sit it out without medication. They felt as if he were passing sentence on them. Surely he could do something to cut it short! They had to get back to their jobs; they had to get Amy better. They felt caught between anger at her illness, fear for her safety, and pressure to get back to work. It was an uncomfortable feeling, not being able to respond wholeheartedly to the obvious priorities of being a parent.

When it was Carla's turn to be at work, she found that she could barely concentrate. Her mind was at home. She felt like a runner about to start a 100-yard dash, poised and tensely waiting for the gun to go off. At any moment she'd have to drop everything and run home. She felt the tug of her two different worlds more acutely than ever before. She realized how protected she had been, by Mrs. Warren, by her mother, and by an adequate day-care situation. It had been so successful until something went wrong. Finally, she could leave, and sprinted home. She rushed in to gather Amy up. Amy was sitting quietly in her crib, sucking her fingers. Carla wept with relief. None of her unleashed fantasies about how sick Amy was were true. And she was there, should Amy need her again.

A Shift of Priorities

Each crisis heightened Carla's feeling that she should be home with Amy. It was becoming almost intolerable to leave her now, especially if anything at all was going wrong. For the first few months back at work, she had been able to avoid these feelings. Now she found her mind on Amy most of the time. She needed to reevaluate her roles. Should she just resign for a while? She knew it would mean a real set-back for her career. But she felt so bad about being away from Amy, and she knew Amy wouldn't be as likely to get ill if she were at home. Jim tried to calm her down, but she got more and more uptight. She called her mother, who suddenly seemed so much wiser than she had ever credited her before. Mrs. Hunt said she thought Carla was missing a great deal by not letting herself be more at home. Could she work part-time for a while? "After all, it's the most important time in any woman's life—the chance to share in your first baby's childhood. It doesn't last very long, Carla." Carla wanted to listen to her mother's rather old-fashioned ideas, but she also wanted to say, "Those aren't our values, Mother!" When she discussed it with Jim, he agreed with her mother. But could they afford to have her interrupt her career?

All of the old turmoil came back. How could she take a chance on her career? Could she learn to work and to mother part-time? She realized she hadn't really learned to mother until a crisis came up. Could she do better now? She knew her work was critical to her own self-image, but now she found that being a better mother was, also. In a way, she dreaded becoming more involved as a mother. She dreaded the isolation, the physical work, but mostly the self-questioning that went with it. If only it were a "clean-cut job," like being a lawyer. Lawyers know when they are right and when they are wrong. In this mothering job, you never know when you're right and no one seems able to tell you. It's almost as if you have to give up a clear sense of identity in order to experiment constantly.

Amy helped Carla make the decision. After the roseola episode, Amy was quite clinging. When she was well enough to go back to day care, she clung fiercely to her mother. Carla had to stay with her each day before she'd separate, just as she did at first. The staff was entirely sympathetic. They urged Carla to stay as long as Amy needed her. One added, "or as long as you need to be with her." Carla felt a sympathetic ear, and broke down to unload her quandary on this understanding woman. Mrs. Thomas, the staff member, nodded as she laid out her misery. She told Carla that most of the working mothers whom she met at the center had the same problem. Each one faced it at a different stage. She thought Carla was right to want to be home for a while—particularly at this time in Amy's life. "Just before she gets too independent." She fortified Carla in her resolve to ask her firm for a half-day job.

After the firm reluctantly agreed, Amy seemed elated each morning. As if she wanted to please Carla, she showed her all her new tricks—cruising around on furniture, going from one toy to another to show her what she could do. She hardly let Carla alone. When Carla tried to telephone, she would interrupt, or get herself in trouble in the next room. When Carla tried to do housework, Amy tried to help her. It took twice as long to do anything, and Carla was used to being rapidly efficient. Now she had to remind herself that she had plenty of time to do what she needed to do and that her time was really Amy's. They began to learn things together. Carla found that she could enjoy sitting on the floor playing with blocks or running a truck across the floor making "truck noises." At first she felt silly, but, as she saw what pleasure it gave Amy, she let herself go. She laughed happily with Amy as she joined in her play. Amy took a real spurt in learning new things. Her faced glowed as if gathering fuel from all the shared times with her mother. Afternoons Carla left Amy at day-care. Amy looked woeful, but waved bravely. She was really growing up, right before her eyes.

The Parent Who is Left Out

Jim could barely stand to hear about the times Carla and Amy had together. Each evening he picked Amy up at the center to bring her home. Amy would cling to him on the way home, but, as soon as she entered the house, would cruise around looking for "Momma." When Carla recounted their mornings together, Jim changed the subject. It was too painful to hear about.

≥ *We filmed a caretaking father with his four-month-old baby in their home. He and his wife had decided that he would be the primary caretaker, since his work could be done at home, while her midwifery took her away all the time. They seemed to be in good balance in these roles. When his wife came home at the end of a long day, he rushed to the door with the baby to greet her. "Darling, let me show you what we've learned today!" She greeted his eagerness with a turn-off, "I'm too tired." As he pursued her, she rushed up to her room without even looking at the baby, to lock her door. He was crestfallen at her lack of interest, parked the baby in the crib, and went downstairs to cook dinner. After she was sure he'd gone, his wife gingerly opened her door, crept out to see the baby, to produce his new achievements for herself. She didn't want to see them done with her spouse, she wanted them for herself. This episode taught us how much competition is normal between parents who care.*

Each parent wants to be involved with the baby's new achievements. It's painful to have to give it all up to the other parent. Jim was reacting in a typical way. If the baby is turning to his wife now, he will react by showing disinterest. The disinterest is really a cover-up for longing to be more involved. Fathers have allowed themselves to be shut out for too long because of this mechanism. It's wise to include them in a way that will make the baby's developmental steps belong to them as well as to the mother.

Negativism

Within a month of her twelve-month birthday, Amy began to be negatively independent. She had started walking all over the house. With her new independence, she again woke up at night, crying out for Carla. Jim rushed to her, in defiance of Carla's objections. She reminded him of their earlier problem at night, but he seemed to "need" to go to Amy. Waking up at two became a regular occurrence. When she woke at six for the second time, Jim brought her in to their bed. Carla objected furiously. Amy, cuddling up to Jim each morning, sensed this.

    ᴥ This kind of unspoken competition over the baby is often a source of a baby's problems sleeping. Carla and Jim had better settle this openly between them, rather than involve Amy. Jim needs to feel more involved and needed.

Amy's independence flourished. She walked around the house chanting "No! No! No!" If her mother asked her to do something, her immediate response was "No!" Then she considered whether she would do it or not. Her first temper tantrum came when she was trying to decide whether to follow Carla to the kitchen or stay with the toy she was playing with. She simply lay down on the floor and screamed. Carla was frightened, overwhelmed. What in the world had she done to set this off? It did not occur to her that Amy had created this dilemma herself. When Carla left her off with Mrs. Thomas that afternoon, she asked whether Amy was showing any of this negativism at day care. Mrs.

Thomas assured Carla that she hadn't yet: "It's still too important and new to Amy. She'll have to test you with it first. She won't act that way here until she's a lot surer of herself than she is now. This negativism is a very important stage in her development."

Carla realized that she would never have been able to take it if she hadn't been at home with Amy as much as she had recently. She would have felt it was "her fault," rather than a natural stage in Amy's development. Now, she could accept Mrs. Thomas's interpretation, could see it for what it was, and enjoy this forceful little girl's newly found independence.

&. *It is very hard for besieged, working parents to have the flexibility and the energy to recognize and enjoy a small child's newly found negativism. The first temper tantrum always makes a mother ask me, "What have I done wrong?" When I interpret it to her, that it comes from within the child, she can feel relieved—if she's not burdened by guilt. When she is working all day and feeling distanced, it must be very hard for her either to tolerate this or to go on to enjoy it. This second year can be a wonderful year, if parents can understand the chaos and resistance as a major development step.*

By the time Amy was eighteen months old she seemed to need Carla less, and it seemed a good time for Carla to consider going back to her job. She felt pressed to return. Amy was delighted with her friends at "school," and Mrs. Thomas encouraged Carla and Jim to leave her all day again. This seemed to work for all of them. The brief respite had made Carla feel much more a part of Amy's life and had given her a deeper understanding of Amy's development. Amy seemed happier about day care now. Jim resolved his jealousy by being much more involved with Amy each evening, and he resumed his "afternoon" at the day-care center.

&. *If there is an "optimal" time for small children to be placed in group care, the second year seems to be it. Toddlers get so much from each other. Their imitative parallel play represents real involvement, and they learn so much from each other that is exciting and rewarding. A toddler at home can be pretty lonely without siblings or peers. I used to keep a list of toddlers in my office so isolated mothers in Cambridge could meet each other to get their children together and relieve the boredom for both parent and child. As they got into more complex behavior in the second and third years, I kept an additional list of "hair pullers," "biters," and "scratchers," so that they could meet each other. A small child starts these behaviors unwittingly and can't understand why other people overreact. An effective solution, much better than punishment, is to get one "biter" together with another. One bites the other, who looks horrified and may bite him back. Both of them look at each other as if to say, "How could you hurt me that way?" And they'll never bite again. To me this is a crucial example of how much small children learn about their own behavior as they play with each other.*

Carla returned to her job with renewed enthusiasm. She had never felt so rewarded as she had by this opportunity to find herself and Amy. Even her skeptical colleagues noticed the energy and excitement she put into her work. She seemed clearer about how to get down to work and how to wind up her day. She had learned a very valuable thing—how to compartmentalize her energy and time.

  & This is a good example of how flexible a workplace needs to be if we want to see it as a backup for a family's development. Women—and men—need to be able to pull back and become available to their families at critical times. Jim should have the same kind of experience his wife had in order to participate in the family's development.*

Toilet Training

The day-care center began to push Carla to let them train Amy. "She's old enough to be trained. All her friends are. We could do it for you."

☙ *Carla immediately bristled with guilt. Were they telling her she hadn't been "on the ball"? She had somehow been gliding along through the second year in her belief that Amy would tell her when she was ready. She knew there was "a time" to do it, and she dreaded it. When the center offered to do it for her, she both felt relief at dumping such an unwelcome responsibility and guilt at her own wish to abdicate.*

She said, "I didn't know it was time to start. You are with her all the time, so you may see signs of readiness in her that I don't. If you think she's ready, I'll start. I want her to do it when she is really ready. So I hope you'll leave it to me to teach her. I feel strongly that it's a parent's job."

☙ *Carla is absolutely right. Parents know their child and their own wishes for that child better than any day-care center, no matter how caring it is. It is an area that can become a very tortured one very easily. It is too important for it to be instituted and achieved outside the context of the parent-child relationship. And, yet, when I've been on the consulting staff of day-care centers, the issue of toilet training is one that is a constant source of struggle between day-care personnel and parents. Quite naturally, the people who must change the child all day are eager for success and they throw up any lack of it at the parents. It becomes an easy area for expressing their competitive feelings. One day-care person, who loved her toddlers and was very sensitive to them, and who also intellectually understood the plight of working parents, said, "You know, when I change messy diapers, I'm hit with the feeling that 'Why isn't this her mother's job? Why am I stuck with doing this mother's dirty work?' Afterward, I'm ashamed of it, but it's there. I hate the job of changing diapers. And yet, I love my toddlers!"*
There are day-care centers that demand toddlers be trained before they will admit them. What edict could be less sensitive to individual pace in toddlers, and more likely to set up failure in this area?

Carla felt herself tighten as she faced the job of training. She knew she should do it soon, and she wanted to do it quickly and perfectly. Suppose she failed?

*The pressure to get such a job done quickly and per-
fectly, which goes with the working mother's need to be "supermom," will certainly contribute to difficulties in this area. I have
written in* To Listen to a Child *about recognizing the signs of
readiness in a child, and times to avoid. The pressures, internal
and external, on working parents is likely to make it harder for
them to wait until the child is ready. There is pressure on them
to get it done quickly—before the day-care center or even peer
pressure enters in. It is hard for them to see the child's side of
it, and that is the key to successful training. Amy must do it
herself.*

Carla and Jim discussed it at home after Amy had gone to
bed. They decided that they were the ones to help Amy get
trained, and that they must follow her lead rather than any of
the advice around them. Carla felt pressured about it, so maybe
Jim could introduce it more easily. Amy always ran into the
bathroom whenever either parent went to the toilet. Jim decided
that maybe he was confusing her by letting her watch him uri-
nate, so he decided to sit her on the pot while he read her a
book. They had their usual delightful time together. So absorbed
was she in their reading games that Carla thought Amy would
never learn what she was sitting there for.

"Who cares?" her father said. "She'll never grow up in our
society without getting trained. Don't get so worked up about
it!" Carla realized that she was feeling pressed and apologetic to
the day-care center. "Whose baby is she anyway—ours or the
center's?" Jim said.

*Jim is putting into proper perspective the pressure
parents feel to have their children be perfect in another setting.
A working mother may have an extra load of guilt and need to
prove to herself as well as to others that she isn't holding her
child back. This is an instance where it really helps to have two
parents.*

With this balance between them, Carla and Jim were able
gradually to corner Amy's interest in becoming trained. She was
so proud of producing her bowel movements in the toilet, and

of staying dry "like Mommy," that it proved to be easier than they had dreamed. Carla and Jim were as proud as Amy was.

Speech

Meanwhile, Amy's speech was developing at a rapid pace. She was able to put sentences together. Although she slurred over some consonants, in general, her words were amazingly well formed. She no longer sounded like a baby. Carla and Jim were terribly proud of her speaking ability. She could converse with them now, expressing real ideas of her own. She was such a little person!

> *Children in day care are likely to speak early and to speak well. There are so many adults to communicate with and so many demands to be made known, that it is necessary to learn sooner. One of the usual reasons for delay in speaking—the situation where everything is done for the baby—is not likely in a center. Also, working parents will push a child to communicate with them when they return at the end of the day.*
>
> *If there is a reason for delay in the child—such as a shy, withdrawn temperament, or one that is easily overwhelmed by a busy environment, or if the child is fearful of not being able to live up to his peers—this will stand out in a day-care center. The additional pressure to speak early may force such a child to defend himself even more.*

Superbabies Again

In Amy's third year, Carla and Jim again began to hear other parents with small children ask, "Aren't you teaching her to read? We are using flash cards and our three-year-old can tell us every letter of the alphabet but X. He can already begin to put letters together in certain words. He can spell out CAT and DOG. You should be working with Amy." In Carla and Jim's social circle, there was a whole culture of young families who were "teaching" their small children. There was a Suzuki method of learning music, a reinforcement method for teaching three-year-olds to use long words, a flash card technique for teaching them letters and ultimately how to read. There was a correspondence course for parents who would sign up for monthly instructiions. The course guaranteed that the child would be reading by four years of age, and "would be better than equal to his peers in cognitive achievements in time for school." Although Jim and Carla had resisted such pressures on Amy before, these questions made them feel panicky that they may have missed an important time in Amy's life for increasing her learning skills. Again they worried that being away all day might have made them oblivious to these apparently important developing skills in Amy.

     ❧ As I mentioned earlier, learning to read is not motivated from within the child. Although all children respond to an adult-oriented reward system, their achievements may not be matched by inner excitement. When time comes for skills like these to be adopted and built upon, the child may be too rigid or may have run out of steam. If children learn later, at a time that is more appropriate for their cognitive abilities, and is motivated more from within, there is no question that it will be a more rewarding experience. Precocity is too expensive.

Carla and Jim's anxieties were based on their peers' expectancies. The fact that they were as busy as they were made them more vulnerable to the feeling of having missed something for Amy. Fortunately, they consulted the day-care center before they made a move. Mrs. Thomas assured them that Amy's biggest tasks at this age were in learning how to cope with others around her and in learning about herself. To be three and in a group setting every day where she needs to get along with other children and to learn about different adults is enough to ask of her. Her parents should be warm and accepting of her at the end of the day, rather than set up a whole new set of hurdles. Carla and Jim were relieved. They didn't want more challenges at the end of the day, either. Amy was such an easy, comfortable child now, and they just wanted to enjoy her. But what would they tell their friends?

❧ *Parents today search for values for their children. The cultural values we used to have have been shot down for us. Nuclear warfare, misuse of our resources, the breakdown of the family—all contribute to a kind of emptiness for parents. They are missing a set of sturdy values with which to indoctrinate their children. We know a great deal about child development, but we don't yet know how to direct parents in their search for meaningful values for their children. It is not surprising that they turn to early education and adultomorphic training programs as a kind of religion. What parents need instead is a respect for the importance of the child's personality and self-esteem, as well as a sense that they have values to impart. We experts need to encourage these as major goals in childhood, rather than anything as superficial as cognitive achievements. Working parents are more likely to be taken in by new fads in the area of child-rearing—not for bad reasons, but because they care so much and want to do all they can to make a good life for their children. They feel that they must prepare their children for the pressures they feel as they work to achieve success in an overloaded life. If parents can become more relaxed about their two roles, pressures on the children may lessen.*

Light at the End of the Tunnel

Carla and Jim are now having a wonderful, easy time with Amy. She is a delightful person and they are thoughtful, caring, and take the time to work out each issue as it arises. It isn't necessarily easy to work and to parent, but they are making it. They enjoy Amy and each other. Their enjoyment will show itself later in Amy's sense of humor and good self-image. When I am not sure how much flexibility there is in a child's self-image, I look for humor and caring for others. Can a child laugh, can she care about others? Amy has both of these. Her peers look up to her, and she is a self-confident little leader already. Carla and Jim are making the best of both worlds—family and workplace. Each side of their lives is bound to enrich the other. There will be more hurdles ahead, but Amy and her parents seem to be ready for them.

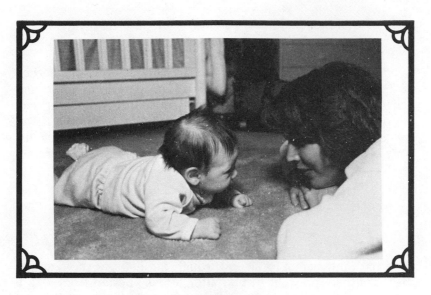

10

The Thompsons

Predictable Problems

᪵ *When a woman who works is a single parent, all of the problems that normally arise seem doubled. Parents with all their energy available for normal developmental problems have the necessary flexibility and sense of humor to face them without tension and anger. But when you are all alone, physically and emotionally tired from a job, every spurt in a child's development becomes a hurdle.*

Being away at work increases the problems that revolve around separation for a single mother. Not only does she long to be close to her child, but when she returns, if she gets satisfaction from her work, she begins to feel guilty that she could enjoy being separate. It frightens her that she might even "want" to be away from a child who has no one but her. Hence, every issue connected with separation—feeding, sleeping, independence—is doubly threatening.

I find that I can predict, for single working parents, when they will create issues that are likely to set up tension. I can predict when sleeping, independence, and feeding problems will surface, because these are universal stresses. But if I can explain them, sometimes the parent can avoid turning them into problems. This is my goal in presenting Alice and Tina's conflicts here.

Sleep

Tina had first begun to sleep through the night at three-and-a-half months. She went to bed after a fussy period from 7 to 9 p.m. and a feeding at 9:30, and could stay in bed until 6 in the morning. Alice felt liberated. Her job was easier, and her life with Tina took on a whole new glow. She felt really rested after eight hours. By four months, Tina went from 9 to 7 in the morning without a feeding or a break.

When she was about four-and-a-half months old, however, she began to wake up screaming every three or four hours, and Alice would rush to her each time. She found Tina only half-awake, crying out briefly, trying to get her thumb into her mouth, thrashing around under the bedclothes. Alice picked her up to feed her, but Tina would take only two or three ounces. She acted as if she weren't hungry, but Alice felt compelled to feed her. She couldn't figure out any other reason for her to wake up. After a few nights, Tina began to cry out until Alice came. When she came, she picked up her half-sleeping baby to feed her. Tina thrashed around until she finally woke up. Then she opened her eyes wide to greet Alice. She began to gurgle and vocalize as if in gratitude to Alice for having come to her. There was no chance that Alice wouldn't come. She was so glad to see Tina again. She had the nagging fear of not knowing what might have happened during the day while she was at work. So *of course* Tina needed her. Aware that Tina was only semi-awake and dazed-looking at first, it did cross Alice's mind that maybe Tina was just dreaming and wasn't really awake. But after she woke up to talk and play, it seemed worth it, an added dividend to see her baby two or three more times. These private times seemed very special to Alice and filled a real need that Alice had.

But these nighttime visits didn't resolve themselves. Instead of lessening, they became firmly fixed—every four hours—at 1:30 and 5 a.m. Alice was getting exhausted. Tina seemed to want to sleep longer in the morning, spoiling their routine of breakfast together. Mrs. Marlin noted how much more fractious Tina was during the day. Also, she said Tina fell exhausted into bed at 10 and at 3, to take long naps. Mrs. Marlin had to wake her up, and wondered whether Tina was getting enough sleep. She urged Alice to consult her doctor. Reluctantly, Alice called me. She had come to depend on these night frolics with Tina. It was as if these nighttime visits together satisfied some need in Alice, and neither she nor Tina wanted to give them up.

As Alice described them to me, they fit into a familiar pattern. The fact that this pattern always began at four to five months had been of interest to me for some time. I had found that many babies, who had already demonstrated that they could sleep through, began at this age to wake up. They needed a little push—to sleep through the night again.

&*In my opinion, it's their new burst of learning about the world that is responsible. Three lines of development are at work here: (1)* cognitive—*babies at this age are suddenly much more aware of all of the stimuli around them, learning about sights and sounds in a new way. Whereas previously they could stick to the task of eating without interruption, now they would rather look and listen than eat; (2)* fine motor—*babies reach out for and capture with their hands, one or both, any object close by, and they want everything; and (3)* large motor—*babies begin to turn over in order to reach out for objects and to get where they want to go. When they turn over in half-sleep, they wake up, and are ready to call for a parent.*

As I questioned Alice, I found out that these developmental spurts had been going on with Tina, that she often turned over in bed at the time she awoke. Should Alice tie her down so she wouldn't awaken? I thought that that wouldn't make much difference.

&*Another factor is more subtle and may combine with these developmental spurts to make such babies awaken on this schedule. Every three or four hours, most of us have a REM sleep cycle (rapid-eye-movement sleep is a very light sleep). In such a REM period, most people come to light consciousness and "discharge" events that happened during the day. Much of an adult's dreaming goes on in such periods. Babies are likely to squirm around, practice newly found motor skills, and cry out or relive frustrations or events from their day. If their activity does not bring them to a wide awake state, they are likely to find ways to comfort themselves back down into deep sleep again. Such comforts may be thumb-sucking, rocking in bed, head-rolling, or clutching a special "lovey" to them. As they get older, they may babble or recount events from the day. If an adult rushes in at this time, she is likely to become a part of the support the baby uses to get from light back to deep sleep. The adult quickly becomes a necessary adjunct to the baby's stretching out from a three- or four-hour pattern to a six- or eight- or 12-hour nighttime pattern.*

There are some children who have a very difficult time "learning" to sleep for longer than one four-hour period, getting themselves down from light to deep sleep. Immature nervous systems—as are found in premature infants and infants who have been through illnesses or other stresses—maintain the four-hour sleep-wake cycle for much longer. Infants who have a hypersensitive, hyperreactive nervous system and a driving, intense temperament are also often difficult babies at night. When I am confronted with a sleep problem of Tina's age, I assess how much of it is coming from the baby and how much is the result of the environment. Learning to sleep at night is an issue of independence. No baby is likely to achieve a mature twelve-hour sleep unless she is allowed to develop independent patterns of getting into deep sleep again after each REM light sleep cycle.

When Alice asked me what to do about Tina's sleep, I needed to explore with her her own feelings about going to Tina at night. I knew that any working mother would feel compelled to go more quickly than she might if she had been at home all day and if she knew the baby had had enough of her already. I knew that a mother at home might more easily recognize the accompanying spurt in autonomy that fostered this sleep imbalance. In Alice's case, I suspected that difficulties on Tina's part might upset Alice's confidence. As a single parent, she might blame herself all too quickly for any upset in Tina. Although a second parent in the home might have his own reasons for rushing to a fussy baby, being the *only* parent leaves one vulnerable to a kind of deep-seated self-questioning that could easily make it harder to let a baby work out her own restlessness at night.

After weighing with her her own reasons for going in to Tina, and Tina's new reasons for coming up to a semi-awake state, I asked Alice whether she wanted to work on this issue. I am pretty firmly convinced that it won't work itself out without mild pressure from the parent. First we talked about the ways Alice *couldn't* do it—"I can't let her just cry it out." "You don't need to, and I wouldn't, either." "But, you mean I should desert her at night? I'd rather sleep with her." "Why haven't you?" "Because I'm afraid of her getting too dependent on me—and me on her." "Those are good reasons for not sleeping with her." Then I asked if Tina had an independent pattern for comforting herself yet. I suggested that Alice stop feeding her every time. "It doesn't sound as if she really needs or wants it. Go to her after a few minutes. Five to ten would give her a chance to comfort herself and to try to get back down on her own. If that doesn't work, then go to her, but don't reinforce her by picking her up. You may be waking her up unnecessarily. Just pat her, or rock her in her bed, to help her get back to sleep. You won't be deserting her in any way, and you may be teaching her patterns for taking care of herself at night. Although this may seem hard now, you may be saving yourself some future grief."

By the time I had finished, Alice was either overwhelmed by my long speech or was trying to digest it. I couldn't tell which, for she was completely silent. Finally, she said, "You make it sound so easy. Dammit, it's not that easy. And I don't want her to grow out of being my baby!"

A week later, Alice called me to say that she couldn't believe it, but she knew that *I* would. It had taken three nights only, and only one period of ten minutes' fussing each night, before Tina began to sleep through regularly. "And she seems relieved!" I congratulated Alice on her ability to take and utilize advice. I told her what I really believed—that Tina was a fortunate little girl.

꙲ *There are a few other techniques for helping to solve this sleep problem, which is a universal one for all single parents and most working ones. One is to prolong the bedtime closeness. Instead of a short ritual, make it a longer one in which you share the events of the day. For a small child, verbal sharing is impossible. But sharing motor and cognitive gains is not. You can help her to get up and down in her crib, praising her for the latter. You can share all the new cognitive and motor gains, but always aim at leaving her in a situation of getting herself to sleep in the end. Sit by her and pat her, or lie down near her, but leave it to her to get to sleep on her own and with her "lovey." A firm resolve is necessary to end the teasing episodes that are bound to result from your being there.*

Waking her up once more before you go to bed can help to interfere with her waking up later. For some reason which I don't understand, your taking control, your breaking into her four-hour cycle by waking her before she wakes you, can be a very effective technique. It should be coupled with the resolve to let her fuss a bit when she wakes up. Just call out to her that you're there, but she doesn't need you.

None of these "solutions" will work unless you are sure, in your own mind, that you want your baby to learn to be independent at night. She'll be ready and will know it, when you are.

There were several times in the first year when Tina began to wake up again. Alice always went to her, and was likely to reinforce Tina's waking pattern each time. Each time, her waking seemed tied to some developmental spurt. Just as she was learning to crawl, she would bounce up and down on all fours in bed, practicing her crawl with each light sleep period. Alice felt she needed to pat her down to sleep.

When Tina began to stand and to cruise around on the furniture, she would pull up on the cribside to a standing position, then call out frantically for help from her mother. Alice found herself back in the same pattern of going to her—every four hours. Again, we discussed Alice's need to go to Tina. She certainly didn't want Tina to feel she wasn't there to comfort her at night. Each time we came around again to the issue of independence and how difficult that was for them both.

As we talked, Alice needed me to back up her resolve. "I know I have to do it. How—without making it too hard on both of us?" I suggested that Alice press a special toy into service—during the day. Enhance the importance of that toy—a rag doll. Whenever Tina is tired or frustrated, Alice could cuddle her and the doll together. She could point out all day that "Dolly" was there, and could be a refuge for Tina. Dolly should become her sleeping companion as well. In order to enhance her value, other toys could be removed, for one toy is much more meaningful than a bedfull. When Alice rocked her and sang her to sleep at night, she could see to it that Dolly was in Tina's arms. Then, when Tina woke at night, she could push Dolly into her arms as she comforted her.

Since the new act of standing seemed to interfere with her quieting down, we discussed that. Tina was so excited about her ability to get up and down all day that it became a pattern at night as well. Except that she wouldn't let herself back down. She'd stand, then act as if she were "caught" in a standing position and needed her mother to help her down. Alice described this: "I'll go to her when I hear her. She'll be standing in her crib, hanging on for dear life, wailing because she's up and can't get back down. I know she needs me to help her down, but as soon as I do, she bounces right back up again! She's only half-awake, so she doesn't even know what she's doing."

I pointed out to her that Tina knew very well how to get down in the daytime. What was special about the night, except that she didn't want to do it alone? If Alice felt sure of herself at night, I suggested that she show Tina in a definite way that she could get herself down at night just as she did during the day. She could hand her "Dolly" and sit by her bed to comfort her until she realized that she could get herself to sleep again.

This pattern of dependency would arise when she was learning to walk, when day-care was too much for her, whenever things were tense for Alice. Both of them would fall back on each other at night. Their need for one another seemed so real that I often felt brutal in my suggestions for pushing them apart. I needed to remind myself as well as Alice that there was a long-term goal involved in a baby's becoming independent at night. Sleep is not the real issue, but independence and feeling self-competent is.

Testing Limits

At the time Tina began to crawl and cruise on furniture, Alice began to find a new crinkle in their relationship. She had to decide when to discipline Tina. Tina used her mobility to explore and then to try out all new experiences. As she explored the furniture, she found the television set and the stove. Both of them had fascinating gadgets to turn. More important, they inevitably got her mother's attention. When Alice rushed over to her, Tina would giggle with delight and collapse in a heap as Alice tried to pick her up. Alice tried to divert her to her toys. She placed barriers around the two forbidden objects. Tina would work at these barriers for long periods of time. They were much more interesting than the toys. Alice found that the harder she worked to find a solution, the more determined Tina became. Tina seemed determined to end each struggle with a showdown. Alice wanted to cry, or give up. Why couldn't they get on like they had before? She felt as if Tina knew very well what upset her and was deliberately making her angry.

Testing limits is a child's way of learning her own boundaries. As Tina tries her mother, she not only tests how far she can go before she must stop, but also tests a new and important area—how can she get along in the face of her mother's anger? By now, Tina knows that, even if her mother storms out of the room, she's nearby, and she can get her back. And yet, Tina is confronted with anxiety when her mother leaves or gets angry. In order to conquer this anxiety, Tina must try it out over and over. In this way, she learns the dimensions of her new independence.

Alice found that she had two courses to follow if she wanted to end such an episode. She could either completely disassociate herself, at which point Tina would lose interest; or she could use strong-arm tactics. If she were really angry or determined, Tina knew it, and she would stop her teasing.

A child who is at this stage learns very quickly about when to stop—when her parent is adamant. She plays on ambivalence and is extremely sensitive to it. If the parent is firm, she knows it is time to give up.

At times Alice had to resort to punishment, even though she didn't believe in it. She had to spank Tina's hand as she reached for the stove. She even spanked her on the bottom, when Tina continued to tease her and to put herself in a dangerous situation. Tina had been following along the electric cord of the television, and Alice had become really frightened when she noticed Tina approach the open socket.

A single parent must do all the disciplining, and it can become very tiresome. When there are two adults to try things out on, it dilutes the job. In two-parent families, if both parents are involved, a baby will begin to slot one parent in the role of disciplinarian for a week at a time and then use the other at other times. If they observe this, parents can see that it's not personal, not "their fault." Alice, being alone, often fears that she's made a monster out of Tina. By the end of a day, she may be ready to run away, or to blow up at Tina. If conflict builds up to the point of physical abuse, it is frightening. More frightening to the adult than to the child. For the child, it may be temporarily painful and worrisome that a parent could be as angry as that, but she has "found her limit" and the incident has served a purpose. For the adult, it may open floodgates of remorse and concern. What if Alice could not contain her anger? Might she really hurt Tina? In these days of so much media coverage of child abuse, every parent is afraid that his or her anger might boil over and that she or he would become an abuser. This is part of caring so intensely. In Alice's case, there is no one else to help put things in perspective. As the sole teacher and disciplinarian, she is finding her way just as Tina is finding hers. It makes discipline a more difficult job—but also a more important one. For Tina must learn about limits and especially about herself as a separate person from her mother.

Tina tried Alice out in many other ways. She couldn't stand having her mother talk on the telephone, try to read, or become absorbed in anything but herself. If Alice was always half-aware of her, Tina could be sure of getting her attention. When Alice started to do anything for herself, Tina would crawl over to pull up on her legs. Or she would start whimpering if she was around a corner. At one time she even cried out as if in pain. Alice came running. When she saw that Tina was teasing, she was furious. She appealed to me, because she was becoming very tense and angry.

I was quite adamant in telling Alice that this was a time to become more detached. I explained that this kind of demanding and clinging often precedes a developmental step toward independence—such as walking. In Tina's case, if Alice could leave her on her own, and stand to have her become more frustrated, she would learn the new step.

> ⅋ *Frustration (if it's not overwhelming) can be a powerful force for learning.*

I urged Alice to let her fuss in the next room, or to let her whimper across the room sometimes. Tina's chance to learn about doing things for herself would be well worth the irritation of hearing her whimper. I also suggested that now was the time for both of them to get out and see other people. Tina would be less bored around others. With a child her own age, she'd learn a great deal, both by imitation and by trying to live up to her.

> ⅋ *Children at this age learn from each other. They learn by imitating whole hunks of behavior. The force to live up to another child is a very powerful one. This is an age when watching themselves in a mirror can be endlessly intriguing to children, but observing another child who has already achieved the task she is working on can be even more exciting. In twins, this becomes very obvious at the end of the first year. One twin will be the observer, the other the actor. The observer watches and watches as the actor tests out the new task over and over. When the actor finally gets close to completion, the watcher stands up and does it. He has put it together by visual imitation.*

Alice listened carefully. She called me later in the week to tell me how well her "contrived" distancing was working. Whenever she became aware of Tina's demands going too far, she would pull out, sit down, and act as if "she were a piece of furniture." Very quickly, Tina realized her determination, and would turn away cheerfully to play by herself. Alice wondered if she weren't as relieved as her mother.

    I am convinced of this. The setting of firm limits at such a time is a relief to the child as well as to the parent. Since the task here is to learn about separating, firm limits serve that purpose for them both.

Alice went on to say that she felt like a fool playing such a child's game, but she could see that it worked. Tina became more actively involved in learning new tasks—playing with simple puzzles, putting one block on top of another and matching the sides, and learning to walk. At eleven months, she had taken two steps by herself!

    Many children are slower than this. They are physically ready before they dare to do it. Alice's encouragement to become independent has driven her on. A feeling of self-competence comes from within, as well as from without. Parents, by hovering, can interfere with this inner force and its fulfillment.

Limit-setting became more and more comfortable to Alice as she saw the success in Tina's face. She told me that Tina had lost the worried look that had accompanied her testing and teasing. The driven quality in Tina's explorations seemed to be lessening as Alice's capacity to set limits grew. I reassured her that the constant need for limits would lessen as Tina more firmly realized her independence by walking, talking, and becoming increasingly able to do things for herself.

    Being the sole disciplinarian of a child this age is a boring job. This is because so much of the time in the child's day is focused around finding limits.

When Tina was a year old, Alice told me this story. She offered it to me as if it were a gift for my having helped her realize Tina's need to become more independent: One rainy day, after a week of rain, both of them were utterly bored with the apartment and each other. Tina began to tease her mother about her food. She threw her food dish down beside her high chair. Alice picked it up and replaced it on her tray. Tina "just happened" to knock it off again. This time Alice told Tina not to drop it off again, and she saw to it that the suction cup was firmly stuck. When she turned her back to get something else, Tina worked hard to dislodge and drop the dish over. Alice was furious, but she contained herself, and even thought to herself how clever Tina was to be able to figure this out. Tina sensed this, and began to get silly. This time she turned the dish over on top of her head. Her mother laughed out loud at this comical attempt to show off. She took the dish away and gave Tina some food on the tray. Tina swept it off. Alice told her "No!" and gently tapped her hand.

     ⁊ Alice could have brought this episode to a close by putting Tina down to end the feeding. But they were locked into this battle by now—as if each got a kind of negative pleasure from it.

Alice tried "one more time," threatening her as she did. She put a few choice tidbits on a colorful plate, trying to distract Tina by pointing to the design. This time, Tina hurled the dish across the room, where it crashed into a glass case, breaking the pane. Alice blew up. She pulled Tina out of her high chair and spanked her hand and wrist several times—in blind anger.

    Then came the amazing result—when Alice picked Tina up to comfort her, Tina looked up at her mother with a relieved look on her face and reached up to pat her mother's cheek. Alice said she felt even more awful than ever about her lack of restraint, until she realized that Tina was thanking her for having finally settled the episode by her firmness.

     ⁊ I am sure that all parents are amazed that a child can be relieved and grateful for a disciplinary action. Until I saw this on my own child's face, I couldn't believe it, either. But their need for limits from outside parallels their effort to learn them for themselves. My own concept of a "spoiled child" is an anxious child. The anxiety is generated by this need for limits—and an

unconscious awareness that they are not available from within. "Spoiled" behavior is most often a kind of searching behavior— searching for limits from adults. When one does interfere with a definite limit, he or she looks up at you with relief, and even appreciation. I urge parents, who are undecided about when to place limits, to watch for this response.

If there is no one around to discipline the child, it leaves the child in a kind of vacuum, searching for ways to deal with the anxiety that is generated. A kind of grim determination invades the child's exploratory behavior. Each task is short-lived, and there is no evidence of any inner satisfaction at having completed it. The child simply goes from one thing to another, trying to provoke or involve the adults around. Self-destructive behavior can follow, as if any reaction from an adult is better than none. This behavior marks the evolution of a "spoiled" child. In a sense, a "spoiled" child is a neglected child. Because it is harder to discipline than to indulge, many parents are unable or unwilling to take this kind of responsibility. Limit-setting can be as vital to a child's development of a secure self-image as are other forms of nurturance. A single or busy working parent will find discipline hardest, being afraid that they haven't the resources to balance the discipline with enough caring. Seeing discipline as a form of giving is a developmental step for a parent. Tina's image of herself or her character will be strengthened, now that Alice has learned to be decisive.

Feeding

Feeding can also be a difficult time for a single, working parent. Feeding a child is such a deep-seated, symbolic act of nurturing that it can serve as an important cementing event at the beginning and end of the day. Alice rushed Tina through breakfast time each morning, dumping her—and her food—off at Mrs. Marlin's and dashing off to work. Mrs. Marlin noticed Tina's sadness and pointed it out to Alice. "Couldn't you set your alarm a bit earlier? Tina really misses that time with you. She looks sad all morning when she doesn't get it" Alice groaned—at her own insensitivity—and began paying more attention to this important ritual—having breakfast together. It softened the separation for both of them.

At the end of the day, when she was tired and frustrated herself, Alice dreaded Tina's disintegration and the teasing behavior that had invaded supper time. She asked Mrs. Marlin to feed Tina before she came to get her. Mrs. Marlin thought about it, then refused. She said, "I'll feed her a snack about four o'clock when she gets up from her long nap. That way she won't be too hungry for you at night. You'll have time to get yourselves together and have a nice, cozy meal together." Alice realized that Mrs. Marlin was acting like a grandmother, looking out for Tina and Alice as a unit together. It was impossible not to be grateful for her advice, although Alice longed for a chance to shed some of the responsibility of feeding Tina. She realized that meals were part of that "quality time" I had told her about. "It isn't the *amount* of time a working mother spends with her baby, it's the *quality* of that time." So, Alice geared herself up to it each day. When she wasn't too tired, she found that Tina was easy. But when she felt hurried or tense, Tina always knew it and overreacted.

At the age of nine months, Tina began to be increasingly terrible to feed. She tossed her head back and forth as Alice brought spoonfuls of mush to her mouth. She put her thumb in her mouth and grabbed for Alice's hand, smearing food all over Alice and the table. She turned her head away. She tried to stand in her chair. Alice felt increasingly angry. She was tired. She had put in a long day teaching and at her studio. She wanted her own supper, yet had to put up with this difficult, negative behavior. In desperation, she held Tina's arms to her sides, then pressed food into her mouth. Tina choked and spit it out. Alice began to weep. Tina leaned forward in her chair, concerned, and reached up to pat Alice on the face. Alice broke down completely, holding Tina in her arms as she sobbed, "What am I doing wrong?"

When she called me, it was easy to make some suggestions that I knew would work. "Give her a piece of toast or a cracker to hold in one hand and a spoon to hold in the other. She'll imitate you with them, and they will give her something to do. She can participate in the feeding. Right now, you are making her too passive. Wear a raincoat if you need to, so she can experiment with her spoon. An even more important strategy now is to let her feed herself soft bits of food. Her pincer grasp of thumb and forefinger is developing, and she'll love doing it. Give her one or two soft bits of food so she can spend some time learning how to pick them up. She'll love that. She'll eat all you want to shove into her while she's occupied with her newest learning skill." These maneuvers worked. They reinforced Tina's new independent skills to eventually feed herself.

❧ From the age of eight months on, a child's goal is to learn to feed himself. If a parent continues to treat him as help-less and passive, his resistance to being fed will grow, and the ingredients of a feeding problem will all be there—unnecessarily. A single, working parent is likely to ignore or to hurry through these signs of independence as long as they're subtle. For a single parent, no one is on hand to observe the struggle, to say casually, "Why don't you let her feed herself?" It's obvious when you think about it. But a harried mother or father isn't likely to think of this as the issue.

In the area of food, although it's easy to say and not at all easy to carry out, a parent must stay out of it. A child will torture you, she will test you, she will win at every turn. Teaching limits in this area is not possible. The only way to limit the struggle is to stay out of it and to play it cool. Food is too important to any parent and a child will know it.

"How can I stay out of it?" asked Alice. "I know she eats a certain amount for Mrs. Marlin, but I want her to eat for me, too. And she needs her food. She's so little. I feel particularly responsible because I'm away from her so much. And yet, on the weekends, she hardly eats at all."

I tried to help Alice to see that Tina is searching for her own identity. In feeding, it's even more important that Tina be in control. We discussed the four basic daily requirements of a toddler and talked about the many detours that are possible if they get into a battle over it. For example, a pint of milk (16 ounces) or its equivalent in cheese, yogurt, or ice cream is important. But even that might become impossible to feed Tina sometimes. Then, liquid calcium could be given in juice or in some other beverage to cover her calcium requirements until she stopped refusing milk products. Four ounces of iron-containing protein, such as a patty of meat or an egg, would cover her iron and protein requirements. If she refused them, she could have an egg milkshake once a day, or an iron substitute could be added to her food. Such vegetables as beans, with a high iron content, might help. But she'd know if you cared what she ate. A multivitamin preparation would cover her requirements for vegetables for any long period of refusal. One ounce of fruit juice or a piece of fresh fruit would cover her Vitamin C requirements. If these four areas are covered in some way—even by substitutes—let the child have her head in refusing everything else.

"But I want her to like food and to eat a rounded diet. That sounds like a pitiful diet to me!" I had to assure Alice that Tina would end this period of negativism toward food herself if it did not become a source of tension between them. Learning to like food and to eat a variety of foods is not a goal at ages two and three. There is a more important agenda for Tina—to learn about her own independence.

I thought Alice had been only half listening. Her eyes seemed to be half shut, and she fidgeted all through our discussion. She said, "You just can't know how hard it is alone. I feel like everything that goes wrong is my fault. Even when you are telling me it's not my fault, like you are now, I can't really believe you. I keep thinking you are just trying to smooth me over. I get so damned angry at Tina that I think I might hurt her. This food bit is the worst. I can remember my own mother forcing food into me and my hating her at the time. I feel so angry and helpless. I swore I'd *never, never* do that to Tina. And yet, I want to so much. I just want her to suffer so she can see how she makes me suffer when she refuses or plays with her food! Here I am being a bad mother all over again. What a terrible life we are setting up together!"

This outburst came straight from her heart, and I knew it. I accepted it and tried gently to reassure her. I knew it was extra tough to be alone, but this strong little girl was a testimony to the success of Alice's mothering. I hoped she could pull back from time to time and see that. Maybe they both needed more perspective on each other now. Had she given up her group of other mothers? It would help to get back with them and share these experiences. Was it time to go over to Mrs. Marlin's and watch Tina in her group? I thought she would see how competent

Tina is in handling herself with her own peers. Did Mrs. Marlin have enough toddlers for Tina? At this age, particularly, it helps to have other children her own age and at her own stage of development to learn from. Toddlers learn an enormous amount from each other. They can test each other, watch each other learn limits. Being cooped up with this lonely struggle is too hard. I urged Alice to begin to develop more of a social life of her own and to work on one for Tina. She and her friends could share baby-sitting. Each could begin to develop times away from the constant demands of child care. The second and third years are a very special time for the child in the area of independence, and backing that up is the most difficult job for a single parent. Now is the time to look for more pleasure and support. Even though it may feel like you are adding a third way-of-life onto an already too-busy first and second, the relief of some social life may be well worth it.

A Single Mother's Doubts

When Tina was three, she was just glorious. She glowed. She had a sense of humor, and she played with the toys in my office eagerly and creatively. One day she was playing with my doll-house as her mother and I talked. Suddenly, in a loud voice, as if she wanted us to hear, she said "This little girl has a daddy, and her mommy doesn't work!" Alice blushed. "Where does she get such ideas? It's as if she were punishing me for all the things I'm not doing for her." We talked about their lives. Alice had begun to see men again. When she brought them home, Tina climbed all over them, as if she were hungry for a man in her life, too. Alice was beginning to feel that she should marry, just for Tina's sake.

    ❦ *This is a poor rationale for marriage. Tina will search for a male counterpart for her mother, in any case. And, in all likelihood, she will find it—in her fantasy, if not in reality. Alice will soon have to talk specifically about Tina's father—what he's like, why he isn't with them, why Tina has never known him. She will need to answer certain questions which Tina will ask over and over as she tries to work out her side of it. Is she different from other children, because she only has a mother? Where is her father? Is he real? What is he like? Does he care about her as a person? Did she do something bad which sent him away? If she tried very hard, could she find him and get him back? Why did Alice need to work? Couldn't she stay home (like other mothers) and take care of Tina? If Alice were smart enough or pretty enough or good enough as a mother, couldn't she get another man for Tina?*

All of this needed airing, so we made a time to talk without Tina. Later, in my office, Alice realized that her guilty feelings matched Tina's questions. She, too, felt unconsciously that she should have completed the family by bringing home a man. She felt inadequate as a person and as a provider of a full life for Tina. She also felt torn between her sculpture and teaching and just being home for Tina. Even as she said this, she hastened to add, "But I like my work. I wouldn't feel complete just staying at home. Good God! What will I do when Tina leaves me? Then I'll really be all alone. And even now, wouldn't I be hovering over her even more than I do if I didn't work? I'd really make her life hell. When you pushed me to let her be independent, the only reason I was able to do it was because I had my work. I guess it's not that I'm struggling with. It's the issue of being adequate as a mother in addition to being adequate to myself. When Tina shows me any little weakness, or a longing for anything I haven't given her, I blame myself for not providing it. I guess I haven't quite come to terms with staying single."

I assured Alice that all mothers who care are in the same boat. Being single makes Alice more vulnerable to Tina's questions and to the developmental problems that are inevitable. Having to work—and wanting the rewards of being a success—adds a sense of guilt to these times, I was sure. Any woman who tries to divide herself in two, no matter how successfully, will feel inadequate at times. How could Alice deal with it? I thought she would have to live with these feelings and to work them out each time they surfaced. Tina and she were doing remarkably well, and I asked if she couldn't take comfort in looking at Tina and in seeing how well-rounded, humorous, and free she was. She was free to express her fantasies and to criticize her mother.

She felt secure enough to do this in front of me, an important stranger. I told Alice to remind herself of her successes in this way.

Each time Alice brought a man home, Tina took him over. She climbed in his lap, patted his face and hair, and treated him so seductively that Alice could hardly stand it. Few men could take it, and many never asked her out again. She asked me how she could ever teach Tina about men. She was afraid to have a male baby-sitter for fear of how Tina might behave. I suggested that she might try to find a preschool where there were men teachers. They are hard to find. Most men are unwilling to work at the pitifully low wages that are paid to caregivers of small children. But it would be an important time for Tina to get to know about men and to feel close to them. Did Alice ever take Tina to see her own father or her brothers? This would be a way to let Tina feel that she possessed male relatives and could count on them. I would certainly want to be sure that she had some male children her own age to play with. We both agreed that it was time to move her to a preschool with more peer opportunities. It would be a terrible wrench for both of them to leave Mrs. Marlin. She had been a source of warm support for them both. Alice was fortunate to have found her.

Preschool

Tina went through a very hard time after the change to preschool. She mourned day and night for Mrs. Marlin. Alice took her back several times, and that helped; but each of them felt the emptiness of missing her. Tina found it hard to get used to so many new children. At first, she withdrew, and it became obvious to Alice that she must take several days off to be with Tina during this transition. This eased things, but Tina still tended to sit in her mother's lap while she was at preschool. This irritated the teachers, and it worried Alice. Was Tina that fearful? As she pressed her, Tina withdrew even more. The teachers looked at Alice as if she were to blame, and she felt completely vulnerable to this criticism.

❧ Being alone is very hard at such times. Alice needs someone on her side, to help her see that this kind of transition is expectable. By her feelings of guilt and anger, and by pushing Tina, she increases the child's anxiety.

The following week, Tina seemed to adjust, but when Alice came to get her, one day at the end of the week, Tina was waiting at the door, nose pressed against the pane, looking forlorn and miserable. Alice's heart sank. She felt as if she had made the wrong move in taking Tina away from Mrs. Marlin. As she gathered Tina up in her arms, the child dissolved into tears. Alice's anger at the new school mounted. She felt like lashing out at them for not being more help to her and to Tina in this transition period.

❧ It is inevitable for a mother to feel competitive with a school, because part of caring is the feeling that no one else can take care of "your baby." This competitiveness is bound to create anger, which is projected toward the school. In addition, Alice feels that the school thinks she's not a "good mother." Being both single and a working mother makes her vulnerable on both counts.

As she sat and rocked Tina, one of the teachers came over to explain that Tina had been fine all day, but had just hurt herself and had rushed to the door to wait for her mother. Tina screamed and pounded on her mother to shut out the teacher's voice. Alice clutched her closer and glared at the teacher, protecting her wounded baby. The scene worsened, and Alice rushed home with Tina, both of them feeling injured and excluded. It was all they could do to get themselves back to preschool the next morning.

❧ Alice could have made it easier for both of them if she hadn't overreacted. Of course, she felt protective, but she added to Tina's temper tantrum. (The end of a long day is a sure time for such a tantrum—with or without cause.) Alice thereby cut off communication with the teachers who might have reassured her and Tina. If Alice wants Tina to be understood and nurtured,

she should work with the teachers, not against them. When a parent takes the child's part without weighing the pros and cons, the child gets a subtle message that the teacher is wrong and the child is right. Alice's vulnerability left her unable to sort out the facts, and help Tina adjust. I hope the teachers will understand Alice's withdrawal and help her with it.

Tina began to balk about going to school. Alice had classes to teach. She felt caught. Should she push Tina to go anyway and to be miserable—or should she cancel her classes and risk her job?

❧ Neither one. She should go to school with Tina in time to sit down with the teachers and help Tina over this period. The teachers would understand, in all likelihood, and could add a little special attention to Tina's day. If Alice stays at home, she is admitting Tina's defeat, and they'll both feel guilty and angry. They'll both be better off if she can tide Tina through the crisis. Perhaps she could come to see Tina at noon. There certainly may be times of crisis when she and Tina will need time off, but this is a time to hang in.

Finally, Alice worked out a way to help Tina. She promised to stay a short time each morning. She began to "woo" one other child Tina's age. She asked this child to supper, took them to a park to play together, and tried to foster a close friendship between them. It worked. Tina and her new friend broke into the group together. By the end of the week, Alice saw that Tina had made it.

❧ In such a period of adjustment, it is even more important that Alice make special times to be with Tina. On weekends, after a long, hard week for both of them, it would be wise to have as few commitments as possible. Then they could both just be together. Alice could devote herself to Tina, and in the process they could feel close enough to talk about what they had been through and would go through the next week. This is a way of preparing for stress, and for mitigating Tina's reactions ahead

*of time. When she overreacts, as she will each morning, Alice
can remind her of their discussion.*

*Raising a child alone and working at a full-time, demanding
job is certainly not easy, but it can be done—and with dignity
and pride. I am sure that a child profits by seeing her parent fill
these two roles competently and confidently. Being able to identify with a mother who is as successful at filling these roles as
Alice is, is a real plus for Tina. She may miss having a father;
she may wish for more of her mother; but she is learning about
strength and coping.*

11

The McNamaras

As Tim began to gather energy and excitement, he became less passive. He screamed for what he wanted. He ordered his brother Daniel around by pointing and grunting. He seemed to sense his family's concern about him and to play on it by becoming more demanding. By seven months, not only was he "king of the roost," he had learned to act the part, too. He was becoming "spoiled."

&. *One difficult part of parenting a child who has been through a worrisome time or who has had an impairment is to press him on to be independent. In the process of nurturing him—to help him catch up—it is all too easy to ignore signs of his becoming "spoiled," overly dependent and demanding of others. Autonomy is the antidote. A child who feels successfully independent doesn't need to order others around anxiously or demand their attention.*

The Need For Limits

As Tim became more active during the day, he got more wakeful at night. He was hard to put down. He made himself stay up until his brother was asleep, and got more frantic and more fussy as the evening wore on. John and Ann felt as if they were at his mercy, but they wanted to give him all they could—to make up for his earlier period of deprivation . . . when they felt they had neglected him. So they let him stay up, but it drove all three of them crazy. Danny got very little from them. As soon as they tried to read to Danny, Tim began to fuss. It seemed impossible to them that Tim was already competing with his older brother.

     ๖ Tim senses their continuing anxiety about him and so is more demanding than he needs to be. Working parents feel their time at home is so short they hate to discipline their children too harshly. And yet, limits are reassuring. A firm hand right now would protect Daniel as well. And it would let Tim know that he was under control. Some of his demands may be coming from his anxiety.

When Tim woke at 3 a.m., if John was home, he was the one who went to him. His ministrations included rocking, feeding, and talking to Tim at length. In fact, when Ann tried to stop him, he said, "This is the best time of the day for me. I get Tim all to myself."

     ๖ Fathers often treasure a middle-of-the-night time with a child for this reason. It may perpetuate the child's waking, but it may also be worth it—for a while.
As we saw in the previous chapters, the issue of sleep is universal for working parents. They need to see the child, and the child may even need to see them, at an extra time in the middle of the night. A child's periods of light sleep, which occur every four hours, stimulate dependency. Sleep is an issue not likely to resolve itself spontaneously (see Chapter 10), and can become a problem. A working family needs sleep to function well during the day.

Ever since Tim had been declared "underweight," Ann's goal was to fatten him up. She fed him every time he gave her a chance. Every time he whimpered, every time he got bored, she popped a bottle in his mouth. By eight months he was not only getting pretty fat, but he was bored with his bottle as well. He would crawl around the house with a half-empty bottle hanging out of his mouth.

&ebdash; *A baby has many reasons for fussing—excitement, frustration, and other intense feelings. These all fuel him to find outlets, to learn, to get involved in the world around him. Using the bottle as a "plug" devalues it as a source of food, and plugging up these feelings cuts down on the kind of intensity he can invest. I would rather see Ann let Tim get frustrated or angry and learn how to settle it for himself. Again, it is difficult for working mothers (and fathers) to tolerate frustration and anger in their children. It is too much for tired parents, and also conflicts with their feeling that a child should be happy for the short time they are home with him. Childhood is not just a time of happiness, however. It is also a time of frustration, of trying to learn all one needs to know in order to become a successful grown-up.*

Sharing Chores and Pleasures

Ann and John worked together to nurture their little family. They shared the housework when John was home. John often cleaned while Ann cooked. As he cleaned, he noticed that Daniel followed him around with a broom in his hand. This gave John the idea of showing Dan how to help. Dan loved it.

&ebdash; *This is a real pay-off in a working family. Children who learn to help and to feel the responsibility of being an integral part of their family's life are preparing for a sharing, contributing future. Too few parents today see childhood as an opportunity for instilling a feeling of responsibility for others. Working parents often take up the slack for their children—partly because it's quicker to do it yourself than it is to show a child how to do it and partly because they would like to spare the child the feeling of having to work. This latter is not in the child's interest. It is never too soon to "learn to work." Work can be play during childhood if it is presented as an opportunity for sharing with parents.*

Ann found that the hardest part of being a parent of two babies and of trying to work at the same time was to figure out how to portion herself out. In a way, she loved getting back to her job, and she wanted to do as well as she could by it. But then when she left work to pick up the boys, she often felt too depleted to be able to respond to them. It seemed as if she were constantly behind in everything she did. She slept badly, ate very little, and was just reaching a breaking point when John came home again for a few days. When he saw how uptight and harassed she was, he asked for a short leave to stay home and help out.

᠅ *John not only saved all of them their sanity—mother's and babies'—but also showed a real sensitivity to the situation. One difficult part of trying to fill two roles well is the lack of enough time. And even if time itself isn't the factor, one has the feeling of never having enough emotional energy to go around.*

John took over the roles of marketing and of transporting the children to and from the center. Whenever he got a chance, Dan proudly showed off "his Daddy." Ann told John about her experiences helping at the day-care center and suggested that he go in for half a day. He was embarrassed. "That's not for me," he said. "You mean it's beneath a man's dignity?" she asked. "You'll get more from it than they will. And you really need to get to know Timmy. Here's your chance!" Ann finally talked him into it, and he went reluctantly to spend an afternoon. It was a dramatic success! Of course, the children were hungry for a man. The caregivers were, too. Everyone in the center perked up visibly. The children chortled as he played with them. Every little face turned his way in the babies' room. And all the three-year-olds in Danny's room followed him around. He was the star attraction, and he loved it. Each time he was home he went back to the center. Soon he began to feel much closer to Tim, and

Danny was ecstatic that his father came "to my school all the time."

    ➠ *A man in a day-care center is pure gold. The children follow him around as if he were the pied piper. The female teachers perk up as if they were getting some sort of sanction for their work. And, of course, everyone envies the child whose father he is. Fathers should take time off more often to attend their children's centers.*

When John told Ann about his day of play at school, she bristled and was about to say, "Well, of course, you didn't have much else to do." But she realized at once that she was just jealous, and so she asked him all about it. As he talked about his time in each boy's class, she saw how much he had missed them. This afternoon with Dan had been like a reunion for them. And, stopping to listen and let herself see what it meant to John and Dan, she could identify with John's getting back into the family.

    ➠ *It is hard for a working parent to see the other parent "at leisure." It calls up all the wishes to be freer, to be able to be with the children at home for them. Ann should resolve to take a day or so off to do the same kind of visiting. It would relieve her anxiety about leaving the boys. In any working family, it is wise to switch roles now and then so that each adult can see how the other one manages it. Also, it is enlightening for the children to see their parents in different roles.*

A Spree

The day before John had to return to the ship, Ann suggested that he keep Dan home from the center and that the two of them go on a spree together. The two "men" went off to the aquarium, had a hamburger, and a game of catch. Danny talked about *his* day with *his* Daddy for months afterward. It became a regular event. Whenever John came in for two or three days, the two of them went on a "toot."

    ❧ I can't recommend this custom strongly enough to both working parents. It isn't the amount of time you save for each child, but the symbolic value you place on it. Have a weekly hour or two for each child in which you are alone with that child, at his service. Not that he'll know what he wants to do with the time, but at least he'll know it's "his." Even if it's only an hour or so, he can talk about it the rest of the week. The child will quite naturally want more time during the week. If it's not possible, you can say, "I can't be with you right now, but remember, we have our time at the end of the week. Then we can do whatever you want. I love that time with you, and it's all ours." Rather than feel guilty all week you can be confident that this kind of special time will make up for a great deal of separation. It's a time to interact one on one, and should not be infringed upon.

After John had left, Ann revived. She felt more loved by John and could see how much he cared about each baby and how much they needed him. She felt equal to anything and resolved that, on his next leave, she would get a baby-sitter to come in so she and John could have time together.

    ❧ A little bit of relief can go a long way. Every working mother should plan a bit of recreation periodically. Somehow, it's the hardest thing to plan for. Not enough time, not enough money, not enough energy—all are excuses for not ever taking time off for oneself. But it can make a world of difference.

Ann's energy and spirits were high for a long time after John left. At the bank, she whistled to herself. Afternoons she danced in to the center, gathering up the children as well as all of the teachers' compliments on John's visit. She found that, as long as she was happy, she had plenty of energy to go around.

Infections

One morning the baby began to sniffle, and Dan came down with a fever. Ann was frantic. What could she do with two sick children. She called the bank to say she wouldn't be in for a few days. They grumbled, but seemed to understand. Both boys, after a four-day bout, recovered, but this was only the first of several such mild infections. The hardest thing for Ann was that she felt "obligated" to get them back to the center, before they were perfectly well and while she still wanted to be with them.

ॐ Recurrent infections are an inevitable part of a group experience for young children (see Chapter 9). Infants are like culture media for germs. They can harbor mild infections, make them stronger, and pass them around a family. I have found that, when there's a new baby in the house, the older children (and adults) usually have to fight off each infection twice. So, employers of working mothers need to be sympathetic to repeated absences.

The difficulty for many parents is that they must return to work while the child is still recovering. If they can take an extra day, that can be an opportunity for a cozy time reading in bed, a quiet time together, a time both parents and children remember forever.

Sleep Problems

Other things happened during Tim's first year that were more difficult for Ann because she was working. Whenever Tim cried out at night, Ann couldn't resist rushing in to him. After one illness, she let him sleep next to her in bed while he was still fussing a lot at night. Every time he whimpered, she would turn over to cuddle and pat him back down to sleep. She realized it wasn't entirely for his sake but that she was lonely, too. When John came back at the end of the week, he quickly put a stop to it, put Tim back into his own crib.

But after John left and she was alone again, she felt a strong temptation to bring Tim back. Danny had picked up on it and wanted to come to her bed as well. When she discussed this with John, he refused even to consider it.

There were several other periods in Tim's first year when he began to wake up again at night. Each time, it seemed to coincide with a developmental spurt (see Chapter 9). At seven months, as Tim was learning to sit and to crawl, and as he was beginning to get around in his world, it happened again. Ann had to use much self-restraint to let Tim work it out for himself at night. Each time he woke up, she had to struggle with her feelings and not go to him right away. She continued to feel cheated out of having enough time with him. John was home one of these times, and it occurred to him that Tim might like a teddy bear to sleep with. Tim loved it from the first. His Daddy gave it to him as a "special" present, and Tim began to cuddle and croon to it. They used teddy as part of the ritual of putting Tim to bed. Whenever Tim was really upset, Ann and John gave him his teddy to hold, as they had held him. Teddy became more and more special to Tim.

      ꒰ The idea of giving Tim a transitional object to help him get to sleep was just the right thing to do. He needed a symbol of his mother's decision to leave him alone at night. Like Alice, as long as Ann was ambivalent or undecided, it increased Tim's turmoil. The teddy bear was, for both of them, symbolic of Tim's need to establish independence at night. Ann needs it as much as Tim does. The marvelous thing to me is how quickly and readily a child will attach to a "lovey." In our culture, it becomes a tremendously important regulator for a small child. We really expect a lot from our babies. Tim can use this symbol as a way of getting himself under control during the day, as a technique for letting off steam or anger, and as a real comfort at night.

At the end of the first year, Ann decided she had to ask the women at the day-care center to postpone Tim's nap until later in the afternoon. Otherwise, he was so tired by the end of the day that he fell asleep before she could feed him or have time with him. Then, about the time she wanted to go to bed, he woke up and was awake all night. If they postponed his nap from 2 to 3:30, he was great at suppertime. She could have her playtime with both boys before their 8:30 bedtime. Time for each of them, as a bedtime ritual, was critical to them all. She let Danny sit beside her for Tim's rock and song. Then she took Dan into her room for his "extra" story and talk, before she put him to bed.

When she was trying to get Tim to sleep through, she found that waking him at 11 before he waked her was a way to break into his cycle of waking. This seemed to get him to sleep longer afterward. And she felt less guilty about letting him fuss awhile before she went to him. The only problem was that she had no time for herself. She was spending the whole evening with her children. She worried more about what it would mean when John came home. Then she'd want more time free to be just with him.

The problem settled itself. When John came home, he took over the bedtime ritual with the boys. He romped and wrestled with them for an hour. Ann was afraid they would get too keyed up to sleep, but, instead, they seemed to be so exhausted afterward that they went down more readily and slept right through. When they did wake to whimper, John kept Ann in bed, and they were able to fall back asleep surprisingly quickly.

⭑ *Two parents can certainly help each other to settle a child's problems. When John is home, Ann's ambivalence is less. The children probably feel more secure with him there, too.*

When Tim began to wake again at a year, Ann knew what was needed—the teddy, plus an extra waking at 11 before she went to bed. This maneuver seemed to give him and her an extra little bit of time together, and he settled down peacefully afterward. Apparently she had conquered their sleeping difficulties before they became a problem.

Feeding

Another area that was to be difficult for Ann in the first year came as a real surprise. She didn't remember many feeding problems with Dan, and wasn't really worried about the children's eating. They were both sturdy little boys, well padded, and cheerful. She equated good humor with good feeding habits.

After being told that Tim was too heavy, she began to be some-what self-conscious about his feeding. She cut back on cereal and fruit and emphasized meats and vegetables in baby foods. After she changed the formula over to whole milk, she cut him back to low-fat milk.

All of these ways of cutting down on calories increase the proportion of protein to carbohydrates and fats. Such ma-neuvers seem to hold a baby's weight in check until he starts moving around. Then his weight is usually no longer a problem.

Perhaps because she had been sensitized to Tim's diet, Ann became more conscious of the fact that he was getting more and more difficult to feed by the age of nine months. He would reach out and try to grab the spoon away from her. He would put his hands into the bowl and smeared food all over his feeding table. When she tried to give him the cup, he grabbed for it, overturn-ing it in her hands. As Danny sang and danced or teased nearby, Tim allowed himself to be completely distractible. At the end of the day, this was too hard for Ann to take. She found herself getting angry at each meal. Tim always got worse when she was in a hurry, it seemed. She tried to get Dan to go into another room at feeding time. She tried to fill up Tim's hands with spoons and empty cups. That worked briefly, but Tim soon found he could throw the utensils onto the floor, creating a loud enough noise to attract Dan's attention and get him back in the room, for more entertainment. Ann got more and more frustrated.

In her urgency to get Tim fed, she missed the point. Tim is bored with being fed. He needs to do it himself now (see Chapters 9 and 10). By eight months, with his new skill—the pincer grasp of thumb and forefinger—all of a baby's boredom can be diverted by giving him bits of finger foods to master. If Ann must feed Tim additional food, she can slide it by him while he's absorbed with his new toy—his fingers.

John came home during one of these feedings. Ann was so frustrated, she ran out of the room weeping, leaving the boys to their father. Tim was so intrigued with his father that he willingly began to eat for him.

&♠ *In families whose fathers are away a lot, the children always do things easily for them and save most of their teasing for their mother. This adds to the mother's frustration. However, it's just a sign of their response to the more novel situation of Daddy's participation.*

After a bit, Danny began to play around, trying desperately to divert his father's attention. John found that, in order to compete for Tim's attention, he had to make feeding a game. As he made faces at Tim, or pretended to feed himself, or teased Tim by offering, then withdrawing a spoonful, Tim was delighted, and he *ate.* Ann turned the feedings over to his father thereafter, but she knew he couldn't be there long. She told him that she just couldn't take time for a long play period around feedings—either in the rush of getting off in the morning or at the end of a long, busy day. They had assured her at the center that Tim ate "just fine" for them. This only irritated her and made her feel less adequate in solving the problem.

&♠ *This is an instance of a day-care center's insensitivity to a working mother's need to be adequate to her children in the reduced time she has with them. She will always measure herself against the day-care center—and find herself lacking. They might have helped her more with helpful hints about what to do with this increasingly irritating problem.*

John hit on the solution. He remembered that Dan had, in fact, been through a period of testing, of throwing food, and they had solved it by turning over some of the feeding to him. As soon as he suggested that she let Tim take over, Ann knew he was right. And he was. Tim chortled with glee when she gave him a few soft bits to pick up. Feeding became a pleasant time again.

By the end of the year, Ann felt she had really come a long way. John was proud of her, and she was proud of herself. She felt that Tim was doing well. Danny was no longer as jealous as he had been. She had been able to hold down her job—even to do it well. She began to learn to save enough emotional energy for them, so that she could balance their needs with her own need to get everything done. And that's one of the hardest but most vital ingredients of mothering—and of parenting in general.

Family Outing

Each time John came home, they planned an outing. Dan would say, "When Daddy comes home, we'll go here—or there." By the time he came home, they all had several options in mind. John slept all of the first day at home. Tim and Dan would play outside his bedroom, waiting for him to get up. When he finally came out, disheveled, he was greeted by four-year-old Dan hurtling himself into his arms and toddler Tim, hungry for his Dad, too. Ann sat back, admiring their reunion.

"What shall we do today?" John's question was magic. He infused energy and excitement into the whole scene. Ann made a picnic while she waited, and John put together the lemonade for drinks and Tim's bottle for comfort at the end of the day. They trekked off to the subway. Each part of the day seemed an extra bonus. Even the subway ride was a thrill when John was along. He held Timmy on his lap and Dan between his legs, pointing out all the pictures on the billboards and the sights through the window when they were above ground. He furnished a whole new view of life.

They went to the ocean as often as they could. Dan wanted to see the boats where his father worked. Tim could say "Boat!" "Wanna ride on boat!" On one occasion, John took them aboard his dragger to "see where Daddy works." It smelled of diesel oil and fish, but the boys and Ann didn't mind—they looked around wide-eyed as John showed off his "boat." He showed them the engine room, silent and stuffy, where he spent his duty time. He showed them his bunk and his locker for clothes. On it were all their pictures. He showed them the messroom where he ate at sea. He took them up to the forecastle where they could each "steer the boat." Later, they took out a rowboat, and John rowed them out into the harbor. Both boys were awestruck, motionless as John maneuvered in and out of the moored fishing boats.

John let Dan try his hand at rowing. Danny took three pulls, then asked to be let off. Tim sat in his mother's lap, quietly taking it all in.

After they returned, and stepped onto the dock, both boys suddenly went wild. All the energy that had been stored up as they had watched John row was suddenly released. They ran round and round the dock until John pulled them up short. Then they began talking. Dan recounted every bit of the experience—with amazing detail. Tim tried to imitate his brother with a few key words. Their constant chatter filled their picnic— neither boy could eat, for talking so much. Ann and John watched them with admiration. They felt close. It was amazing that they could be so busy, apart most of the time, and yet could get together at times like this when, in such a short time, their world seemed complete.

12

The Problem of Time

A difficult problem in a two-career family, one that underlies most other difficulties, is time. There is never enough of it—no time for emergencies, no time to handle added stress, no time for joy and the extra pleasures of just being together or of being alone. The descriptions two-job families give me of their days and nights leave me out of breath. Precise timing and compartmentalization is critical each day. Are we all too busy?

When I discharge teenagers to "adult" doctors I always ask them first what they remember about being a child. Since they know me so well, they often unload some very searching memories. The children born in the fifties remember the fact that "no one ever smiled when I was little." I was horrified, and learned that they saw their parents as too serious, always wondering whether they were doing the right thing in their role as a parent. I fear that the same memories may dog children of the eighties. "No one ever smiles at our house" is a common complaint now. Everyone is too busy. There is likely to be no leeway for humor, for fun for its own sake.

and have fun—a romp with the children. A child's day is likely to be contained and organized if he or she is in group care. A child needs to blow off steam as much a parent does. A really physical time together may well end in tears, but children need to blow up that way. After the excitement and the tears, a lovely, low-keyed cuddle with a story or a book brings everyone back together again.

"Quality time" is the latest buzzword. Every working parent asks me to define it as if it were a magical entity. It's not. It is a label for the kind of warm closeness that happens all too rarely in any highly scheduled day. Mothers at home all day rarely remember such times. Children who have their parents with them aren't likely to be aware of special "quality times." Since a working parent feels torn away for such a large part of the day, she may put too much emphasis on "quality time" to make up for her absence. The harder she tries, the less likely it is to happen.

As a very busy father, I always wanted to gather my children together when I finally made it home at night. They were exhausted, too, and ready to fight with each other. They had other agendas, such as homework and telephone calls to their friends. They wanted to see me, but not on my terms. My idea of "quality time" was too artifical, too much of a "party event." As I tried to pull them to me, "herd" them together into an assigned room, it felt to them more like what they had been through all day. They came, reluctantly, for my "quality time." But when I waited, leaving it up to them to come to me one at a time and at their own pace, we had a lovely, intimate time together. I learned finally to read to each one alone and to save a bit of time at bedtime so that we could just relax and gab after their story. At that time it seemed much too low-keyed to me. Now I realize that these brief moments were our "quality time." These only come when adults and children are ready.

If everyone in the working family does his or her share, time together is increased and enriched. Just as fathers begin to expect to share in household chores, so must children be taught to participate. This may be the best dividend for the children of the eighties. If they learn to share in the workload, if they are expected to feel and to share responsibility, they will be far ahead of most American children of the past few decades. The "ME" generation is a blot on our society, largely because children of affluent and upwardly mobile families were never taught to assume responsibility for others around them. At first, this will seem to require even more time. A parent must be prepared to start teaching early. Even toddlers can be taught to set the table, and they will love it. Three-year-olds can participate in washing dishes or in folding clean clothes. They will proudly display their prowess. While teaching these skills takes valuable time and patience at the end of a busy day, it can be "quality time," if the work is presented as an opportunity rather than as a chore. Children of this generation will be ready for less stereotyped sex-roles if they are exposed to mutual participation in the family.

The myth of Supermom and Superwoman constantly drains the energy of a working woman. Men, as well, who are more actively involved in the family, may feel they should be perfectionists at home just as they are in the workplace. This attitude is no help in adjusting to the different demands of the two areas. It only leads to a guilty feeling that neither job is really getting done, adding more pressure to an already pressured situation. I advise two-role parents to see these years of stress with small children as temporary, short, but very important. Your job may have to wait for your very best efforts, and you may have to find ways to postpone or dilute your ambitions, until parenting becomes less demanding. You need time and energy to be the kind of flexible, attentive parent that you want to be. Parents who save some part of themselves for the family at the end of the day and the end of the week feel more rewarded. The children's lives at home are limited, and it is on these early years that they base their self-image. Unless you have time and humor to listen to your child's side of each daily event, you too may be remembered as "never having smiled."

Every task—feeding, going to bed, getting dressed and undressed—can be a time to interact positively with your child. It can be a time for sharing feelings, for talking together, for laughter, even for argument. A child's goal may be independence; a parent's dependence or learning. They may clash, and just as much strong feeling is conveyed in a clash as in a more positive interaction. But when a parent and child have too little time with each other, it's more painful to clash. After an argument or a punishment, it helps to pick the child up, sit down, and pull it all together again by discussing what has happened.

As we saw earlier, fostering independence may be one of the hardest things working parents have to face, for they may not see the issues as they arise. Discussing a child's development with a child's caregiver at home or at day care should be a regular event, and will help keep you alert to newly developing independence.

Keeping in touch with children's day care, nursery school, or social life may add extra time onto an already overloaded schedule, but it is essential—for you and for them. It gives you a chance to see where they are in relation to peers, new skills, and other adults. It will give you the assurance that they are not suffering too much from your hectic life. Parents who are working need to know that their involvement outside the home isn't creating problems for their children.

For the child, your expressed interest in his or her day and social life is a real support. Children who feel this interest have more confidence in themselves. They have an important audience to show off for and to live up to. They can bring home their feelings and frustrations because they know you are interested and involved. As children get older, they may express resentment at your involvement, but it is certainly better to have a parent to rebel against and to resent than to have one who is uninvolved.

Minor childhood illnesses can be special times for parents to treasure. They are times when the child can regress and be taken care of. Working parents should save up their sick leave so they can take a day at home with a sick child. Everyone remembers childhood days of being curled up in bed, under soft warm covers, being read to or coddled. "Don't you want some more hot tea? How about some broth or juice now? Can I read to you? Do you want to play a game?" Any time one feels bad or vulnerable, these memories come back, and one longs to be sick in bed again with a caring adult hovering over. Every busy, working parent should see to it that they set up some of these memories for their children. After returning to work, telephone your child from time to time to see how he or she is feeling.

Plan vacations as family events as much as possible. These blocks of time together are special, especially for working families. But don't overload them. They can become so full of activities that they duplicate the overloaded lives that working families lead the rest of the year. A cozy, relaxing time together may be more rewarding than one that is too heavily planned.

Shared weekend rituals are especially important in working families. Going to church, going to Grandma's, going to a movie, shopping together—all of these become happy memories later on. Planning the week together makes both parents and children feel involved with each other and responsible for getting the work of the family done. A child who shares in both the fun and the chores is bound to feel more valued, more grown up.

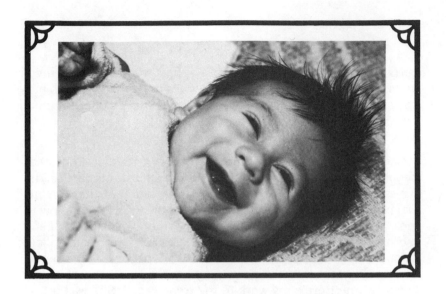

EPILOGUE
Sharing the Joys

&. *Can working families find time and energy for joy? Certainly there is satisfaction in the day-to-day survival, the achievements of accomplishing two jobs. But what will make it feel like it's all worth it? Certainly, children won't feel that way if everyone in the house is hurried, harassed, and worried.*

How can it become a joyful time of life? First of all, slow down and look around. If you are having a good time with your job, share that with your children. Talk about your work and its rewards. Let them meet your colleagues and see how you do what you do. If they can identify with you in that role, too, it will be doubly rewarding for them. As soon as I began to let my children come to my office to see their friends, whom I treated, and to meet the many other small children I take care of, they began to want to "help Dad out." They came to play with the children in the office "to make up for all the things you were doing to them, Daddy." But they also began to observe and to remark on children they saw on the street. They began to ask questions about child development and about why mothers and fathers do what they do. They became "child development ex-

187

perts" in class. Other kids who were baby-sitting would call them at home to "get their advice." Sometimes they would turn to me, but often they would figure it out without me. I could see how much sharing my job with them meant.

Carla took Amy to work when Amy was a toddler. The other people in the office hovered around this beautiful little girl. The typists let her type. The office boy took her with him on his errands. The other lawyers showed her how to draw and how to look at their big books. Amy never forgot "her work." Each morning she packed her own "bweefcase." She took an old satchel of her mother's and stuffed it full of papers. At the center she would strut into the room, crying out to all the children, "Look at me. Here's my work in my bweefcase!" She was proud when her mother came to get her at the end of the day—proud that they could carry their briefcases home together.

   ❧ If you can stop being a Supermom or Superdad now and then, the joys of sharing, of watching your child identify with you, can soften up the stress of working while parenting. Watching a child develop along each developmental line is something not to be missed. Each new step is such a pleasure—for them and for you. How about having your children help you cook breakfast on Sunday? He can stir, she can set the table, they can both help. And then you might try a game: "Now let's hurry like we do every day—rush, rush, rush—finish your toast— where's your mitten? Whew!—Isn't it fun when we have time to make a nice breakfast? You are such a help to me." Watch them puff up with pride.

Jim was the most adept at getting Amy into a joyous mood. When Carla and Amy arrived home, weary at the end of the day, Jim waited behind the door. As they entered, he leapt out at them. Both serious females jumped. Amy almost started to cry. Jim grabbed both of them into his lap and hugged them. As they caught their breath, he began tickling them. They all ended up giggling and chasing each other around the house. By the time they finally subsided and sat down with each other, they were all in a happy mood. Amy thought of her father as the "funny man." He was a morale-booster for them all.

&. *Fathers who are involved from the first are bound to feel more rewarded by everything that happens in the family. Every new step the family achieves or the child achieves feels to them like part of their efforts. The conscious sharing of roles in families today will pay off for children in the future. Boys will "know" and not question their cooperative roles in the next generation. Girls will "know" that men can be, and will be, nurturant and supportive. Children have a richer experience in working families that are successful in sharing their many roles.*

Working parents who see their role at home as a balance to their working life find all sorts of other joys and compensations. What a pleasure it is to be home, safe together, snuggling with each other after a terrible day. Christopher Lasch calls the family a "haven in a heartless world." Indeed it can be—for adults as well as for children. The reward of being able to sit and watch the new achievements of a small child, to share in his joy at the new step he's just taken, is a proper balance, say, for having pulled off a precarious bank merger.

As we saw with Alice and Tina, since a working parent is likely to be tired or distracted, he or she may be less likely to hover over children at times when they need independence. If parents can allow themselves to sit back as observers while the children make their own decisions, the joy will come in watching them deal competently with the outcomes of their own decisions.

Ann McNamara worked very hard so she could be at home when her boys came in after "school." She finally arranged her work schedule so she would arrive just before they did. John went to get them when he was home. Ann was sorely tempted to start the housework as soon as she arrived home. So many things were left undone, and she never had time to do them. But then she reminded herself that she made all these arrangements so that she could be at the front door when they came in. One day, as she heard steps on the porch, she also heard a small voice saying to his father, "My mom thinks we are special. She's home before we are just so she can hear our news." As she picked each one up to hug him, her eyes were teary. The boys, bursting with energy, were ready to talk, and sat down next to her on the sofa to "tell" about their day. John sat across from them, admiring his handsome family. Each boy blurted out his "news." Danny and the baby fairly fought to be first. Each time one would start, the other would burst in with *his* news about his "work." When Tim got his chance, he stuttered with excitement and couldn't produce a single word. Danny helped him remember. Finally, they were both spent. Danny turned to his mother and said, "It's your turn. What was news at your office?" John and Ann looked at each other, sharing the realization that these boys were growing up with a real awareness of others. Working and raising children wasn't so bad after all. Everyone could make it—and make it work well.

* *The ultimate reward is when your children grow up into balanced, flourishing individuals who identify with both sides of you—the working and the caring.*

REFERENCES

Auerbach, S. *Confronting the Child Care Crisis* (Boston: Beacon Press, 1976).

Bell, D. *Being a Man: The Paradox of Masculinity* (Lexington, Mass.: The Lewis Publishing Co., 1982).

Bettelheim, B. *Children of the Dream* (New York: Avon Books, 1969).

Bowlby, J. *Attachment and Loss*, Vol. 1 (New York: Basic Books, 1969).

Brazelton, T. B. *Infants and Mothers*, Rev. Ed. (New York: A Merloyd Lawrence Book/Delacorte Press, 1983).

Brazelton, T. B. "What You Should Look for in Infant Day Care," *Redbook* (February 1982).

Brazelton, T. B. *On Becoming a Family* (New York: A Merloyd Lawrence Book/Delacorte Press, 1981).

Caldwell, B. M., and Freyer, M. "Day Care and Early Education." In B. Spodek (ed.), *Handbook of Research in Early Childhood Education* (New York: The Free Press, 1982).

Daniels, P., and Weingarten, K. *Sooner or Later* (New York: W. W. Norton & Co., 1982).

Dixon, S.; Yogman, M. W.; Tronick, E.; Adamson, L.; Als, H.; and Brazelton, T. B. "Early Social Interaction of Infants with Parents and Strangers." Paper presented to the American Academy of Pediatrics, Chicago, Ill., October, 1976.

Field, T. M. "Effects of Early Separation, Interactive Deficits, and Experimental Manipulations on Infant–Mother Face-to-Face Interaction." *Child Development* 48 (1977): 763–771.

Freud, A., and Dann, S. "An Experiment in Group Upbringing." *Psychoanalytic Study of the Child* 6 (1961): 127–168.

Galinsky, E., and Hook, W. A. *The New Extended Family: Day Care That Works* (Boston: Houghton Mifflin Co., 1977).

Goldberg, S. "Social Competence in Infancy: A Model of Parent–Infant Interaction." *Merrill Palmer Quarterly* 23 (1977): 163–177.

Greenfield, P., and Tronick, B. *Infant Curriculum* (Santa Monica, Calif.: Goodyear Publishing Co., 1980).

Greenspan, S. I. "*After the Baby: The Best Time to Go Back to Work.*" *Working Mother* (November 1982): 95.

Heins, M.; Stillman, P.; Sabus, D.; and Mazzeo, J. "Attitudes of Pediatricians toward Maternal Employment." *Pediatrics* 72 (1983): 283.

Hoffman, L. W. "Maternal Employment and the Young Child." Minnesota Symposium on Child Psychology, 1982.

Howell, M. C. "Effects of Maternal Employment on the Child." *Pediatrics* 52 (1973): 327.

Howell, M. C. "Employed Mothers and Their Families." *Pediatrics* 52 (1973): 252.

Klaus, M., and Kennell, J. *Maternal-Infant Bonding* (St. Louis: C. V. Mosby Co., 1976).

Klinman, D. G., and Kohl, R. *Fatherhood USA* (New York: Garland Publishing, 1984).

Norris, G., and Miller, J. A. *The Working Mother's Complete Handbook* (New York: E. P. Dutton, Sunrise Books, 1979).

Parke, R. *Fathers* (Developing Child Series) (Cambridge, Mass.: Harvard University Press, 1981).

Pederson, F. A., and Robson, K. S. "Father Participation in Infancy." *American Journal of Orthopsychiatry* 39 (1969): 466–472.

Piotrkowski, C. S.; Rapaport, R.; and Rapaport, R. "Families and Work, an Evolving Field." In M. Sussman and S. K. Steinmetz (eds.), *Handbook of Marriage and the Family*, 2nd Ed. (New York: Plenum Publishing Corp., 1984).

Pizzo, P. *Parent to Parent: Working Together for Ourselves and Our Children* (Boston: Beacon Press, 1983).

Provence, S.; Naylor, A.; and Patterson, J. *The Challenge of Day Care* (New Haven: Yale University Press, 1977).

Seashore, M. J.; Liefer, A. A.; Burnett, C. R.; and Leiderman, P. H. "The Effects of Denial of Early Mother–Infant Interaction on Maternal Self-Confidence." Prepublication draft abstracted in *Infant Care*.

Sullivan, S. A. *The Fathers' Almanac* (Garden City, New York: Doubleday and Co., 1980).

"Toward a National Policy for Children and Families." Advisory Committee, N.R.C. National Academy of Sciences, Washington, D.C., 1976.

Trost, J. "A Study of Men's Behavior and Views." Swedish Information Service, Swedish Consulate (825 Third Ave., New York, N.Y.), 1983.

"Who Will Mind the Babies?" National Center for Clinical Infant Studies, Washington, D.C., 1984.

Index

The Author

T. Berry Brazelton, M.D., is Professor at Harvard Medical School and chief of the Child Development Unit at the Boston Children's Hospital Medical Center. The Brazelton Neonatal Behavioral Assessment Scale is in use in major hospitals throughout the United States and abroad. Dr. Brazelton was awarded the prestigious C. Anderson Aldrich Award for Outstanding Contributions to the Field of Child Development. He is President-Elect of the Society For Research in Child Development. Aside from his numerous scholarly publications, Dr. Brazelton is well known to parents as a contributing editor of *Family Circle* magazine and as the author of *Infants and Mothers, Toddlers and Parents, On Becoming a Family,* and *To Listen to a Child.*